5·24·12   57601   30.16
YBP

D0072795

THE REAL
CHANGE-MAKERS

THE REAL CHANGE-MAKERS

Why Government Is Not the Problem or the Solution

DAVID WARFIELD BROWN

 PRAEGER

AN IMPRINT OF ABC-CLIO, LLC
Santa Barbara, California • Denver, Colorado • Oxford, England

Library of Congress Cataloging-in-Publication Data

Brown, David Warfield.
  The real change-makers : why government is not the problem or the solution /
David Warfield Brown.
     p. cm.
  Includes bibliographical references and index.
  ISBN 978-0-313-39774-5 (hardcopy : alk. paper) —
ISBN 978-0-313-39775-2 (ebook)
  1. Social problems—United States. 2. Social ethics—United States.
3. Problem solving—United States. I. Title.
  HN57.B6583   2012
  320.60973—dc23   2011035379

ISBN: 978-0-313-39774-5
EISBN: 978-0-313-39775-2

16 15 14 13 12   1 2 3 4 5

This book is also available on the World Wide Web as an eBook.
Visit www.abc-clio.com for details.

Praeger
An Imprint of ABC-CLIO, LLC

ABC-CLIO, LLC
130 Cremona Drive, P.O. Box 1911
Santa Barbara, California 93116-1911

This book is printed on acid-free paper ∞

Manufactured in the United States of America

Contents

Acknowledgments

My work here reflects what I have learned on an intellectual journey begun some 30 years ago. I have shared that journey with many friends, staff associates, colleagues, and students, and their influence permeates this book. That is how it should be because the spine of my argument throughout is that interdependence is unavoidable and to be welcomed.

The influence of those I want to acknowledge here goes back to my political campaign and government days with Congressman Ed Koch on whose staff I served and from whom I learned so much about how government works and, at times, doesn't work. Then there were my colleagues at the Rand Corporation whose research contracts with the City of New York were valuable, but vulnerable, as the city encountered an unprecedented fiscal crisis. From Rand I joined the New York State Commission of Investigation as its chairman and discovered that a bipartisan team of fellow commissioners, along with staff, could get a lot done when pursuing investigations across the state where government had miserably failed to serve the public interest. Then my friend Ed Koch, the newly elected mayor of a city still in fiscal distress, asked for my help in putting together his city administration. It was a difficult decision for my wife and me, but I joined Ed, moved the family back to the city, and rounded out my education in how government works and doesn't work.

In City Hall, I learned not only from the mayor but from many of those who served in his administration including Bob Wagner, Jr., Ronay Menschel, Phil Trimble, Judith Friedlaender, Phil Aarons, Maureen Connelly, Peter Solomon, and Diane Coffey. With my children Sarah and

Peter at an age when I wanted to share more time with them, I put my decade of full-time government service to one side and moved on to teaching and writing. A former Rand colleague, Art Swersey, suggested I do some teaching at Yale's School of Management, and his colleagues welcomed me knowing that my government experience was something I could offer that most of them could not. For a time, I also kept my hand in the public sector as a board member of the New York Metropolitan Transportation Authority, whose chairmen, Dick Ravitch and then Bob Kiley, were examples to me of how the public good can be served without compromising personal standards.

At Yale, I learned a great deal from both my graduate students and faculty colleagues about the culture of professionalism we had all become immersed in. Colleagues like Sharon Oster, Sid Winter, Ted Marmor, Paul Bracken, Garry Brewer, Greg Dees, and Doug Rae, and students too numerous to acknowledge here, shared valuable insights with me about such a culture. I began to examine it more closely in my classrooms and write about it at home with my children close by. During a decade of teaching and writing, I also reached out to those scholars who could help me better understand how higher education shapes the professional mind-set. David Riesman at Harvard and Lawrence Cremin at Columbia Teachers College both educated me and served as mentors, which led to my accepting the presidency of Blackburn College.

Larry Cremin also put me in touch with the Kettering Foundation and its president, David Mathews, who would later invite me to be a visiting scholar after my tenure at Blackburn College came to an abrupt end when my wife, Alice, became ill—a condition David Riesman told me was all too common among those married to college presidents. The two years, however, that Alice and I shared in helping Blackburn get back on its fiscal feet was a day-to-day experience that better informed my sense of how members of a community can come together when the going gets tough. There was Mim Pride, who succeeded me as president, Norma Dunn, Sam Meredith, Jan Zimmerman, Mark Armstrong, Ren Draya, and so many other faculty members and students.

Early on in my work with Kettering, a monograph of mine on social conventions was further developed by Adam Bellow at the Free Press, who saw my work on everyday coordination problems and practices as a welcome departure from the liberal reflex of turning to government for solutions. The manuscript, *When Strangers Cooperate*, was, like this one, indebted to the political economists Charles Lindblom, with whom I consulted at Yale, and Thomas Schelling, whose *Micro-motives and Macrobehavior* has been of lasting importance to me. Why? Their work was not tethered to strict methodologies but rather came from their shrewd observations and experience of the everyday world. Their influence and the "storytelling" work of social psychologist Karl Weick have informed both my teaching and writing to the present day.

After *Strangers* was published I rejoined the academy at the New School's Milano Graduate School of Management and Urban Policy. It brought me back to New York City where I first learned what governments do and what citizens can do. My faculty colleagues and the students at Milano further shaped my interest in social problem solving, which I continued to develop in the classroom and in my work on various committees. So many colleagues left their mark on me: Rikki Abzug, Bob Beauregard, Ed Blakely, John Clinton, Alec Gershberg, David Howell, Aida Rodriguez, Bryna Sanger, Alex Schwartz, Tatiana Wah, Mary Watson, and many others across the New School. There was also the continuing influence on my work of game theory and the complexity research of the Santa Fe Institute. For me, the elegance of such models has not simplified explanations of how things happen but instead challenged various disciplines to reconsider their assumptions. And I have always welcomed such apostasy.

Over the years many have shared with me their experiences in government, higher education, and elsewhere that convinced me that the *social dimensions* of problem solving are paramount. I think of Parker Palmer, John Chandler, Frank Macchiarola, Burt Malkiel, Neil Rudenstine, Allen Holt, Peter Goldmark, Steve Berger, Earl Brydges, Jr., Eric Seiff, David Lyon, Matthew Nimetz, Suzanne Morse, Lloyd Morrisett, Richard Wood, Donna Shalala, Patricia Graham, Robert Reich, Jim Fallows, Charles Peters, Ken Auletta, Geoff Hazard, Norman Dorsen, and John Gardner. David Mathews, with whom I have had a continuing intellectual relationship and loyal friendship for the past 25 years, deserves special mention here. As a former president of the University of Alabama and secretary of the Department of Health, Education, and Welfare in the Ford administration, David and I shared similar crossroads of public and private institutions. Over the years David greatly influenced my thinking about the importance of democratic self-rule and how many of our institutions frustrate or neglect the potential of citizens to do more for themselves and their communities.

There have been others at Kettering from whom I learned and with whom I shared my intellectual journey: Debi Witte, my coeditor for almost 20 years of Kettering's annual publication, the *Higher Education Exchange* (*HEX*); John Dedrick, who included me in the work of the Foundation focused on community educators; and Derek Barker with whom I coedited *A Different Kind of Politics* using the interview form of inquiry that I developed over the years for *HEX*. So many of those I interviewed contributed to my understanding of what David Mathews and Kettering highly value—deliberation among equals—as well as helping me learn more about "public work" from Harry Boyte; about "public journalism" from Jay Rosen; about "public scholarship" from Noelle McAfee, Julie Ellison, Jeremy Cohen, and Scott Peters; about "democratic partnerships" from Ira Harkavy, John Wheat, and Marguerite Shaffer; about "public making" from Doug Challenger and Joni Doherty; and about the culture of professionalism in higher education from David Cooper, Peter Levine, Adam Weinberg, Mary Stanley, Claire Snyder, Al Dzur, Mike D'Innocenzo, and KerryAnn O'Meara, among others.

I should also acknowledge my former agent, William Clark, who helped me improve what I foresaw to be this book, and, of course, Valentina Tursini, my editor at Praeger, who brought the whole project home with her enthusiasm and practiced care.

Last, but not least, is my wife, Alice, with whom I have shared the journey and to whom this book is dedicated. What can I say but that love sustains when so much else does not, and our son Peter and daughter Sarah enlarge that circle of love as does my brother Coleman, whose exemplary life has taught me many things.

It has been a long and eventful journey of discovery with so many contributing so much to what is now mine alone to offer here.

Introduction

The young surgeon in the emergency room asked me, "Why, Mr. Brown, do you rollerblade?" I looked up at him, "Hey, I'm 64 and I need the workout." He looked down at the deep gash in my forehead and laughed, "Don't you think you should act your age?" Then I laughed, "Over my dead body!" He paused and finally said, "That's what I'm talking about," and, as we both laughed, he started sewing me up. A bad tumble, however, has a strange way of clearing the head, of reducing one's thoughts to essential things like standing up, lying down, and getting through the night. And that's when I first had the idea for this book—in the middle of the night.

I thought back to when I took leave of the in-charge world and the practice of law in New York City, having lived this book, long before ever conceiving it, as a young lawyer on Wall Street, counsel to a congressman, chairman of a state investigation commission, deputy mayor of New York City, board member of a public authority, and law firm partner. I considered calling my mother and asking only half in jest, "Can I go now?" After all, what mother doesn't want her son to be a professional? Still, I remember that mine was wise enough to warn me, "Be careful what you want in life, David; you might get it." All I knew was that my professional life left something to be desired. It is similar to when a salesperson in a bookstore asks me: "Can I help you?" I usually reply: "No, thank you. I don't know what I want until I find it." So after leaving the in-charge world, my subsequent teaching and writing and a stint as a college president helped me to discover and embrace the idea that everyone counts—not just those in charge or those with professional credentials. A dangerous immodesty persists among those who are ostensibly in charge and the analysts and experts who advise them. I think much of this hubris, as did mine, comes from their education and socialization as professionals, a mind-set that can be profoundly anti-democratic when presuming that one's professional knowledge and experience is a sufficient substitute for a democratic process of participating equals. To make matters worse, the average citizen can also think this way when entrusting so much of the public agenda to professional hands. Too many are too busy taking care of personal business assuming that professional surrogates somehow can fix things for them. It isn't going to happen.

For a moment, I thought I would simply title my manuscript *Silly Nation*. Silly nation—where too many citizens seem content to let our public world become a spectator's arena for watching the politicians, pundits, and talking heads perform. Too many seem all too ready to fault government for doing too much or too little but rarely point the finger at themselves. Such an attitude is beset with contradiction when assuming that those in charge can solve our social problems—failing health, failing to educate, failing those in greatest need—especially when governments, at whatever level, now find themselves badly strapped for money. Nonetheless, having become couch potato citizens, many sit back putting down government but at the same time putting up with it.[1] Like the proverbial drunk looking for his lost keys under a street lamp because the light is better there, too many look for answers or scapegoats for our social problems in the well-lit precincts of our very visible government institutions. It is the territory that the media stakes out in its 24/7 preoccupation for "news," conditioning some couch potato citizens to believe that certainly the keys they need are there—somewhere.

Despite fiscal deficits as far as the eye can see, some folks prefer to keep top-down government at the center of things. It serves their interests. Professional politicians see us as essentially voters to be wooed and won over. Special-interest advocates solicit our petition support and donations but little else. To pollsters and experts on call, we are a database and clientele in need of their analyses and forecasts. To the 24/7 media crowd, we are consumers of their news and their opinions, but, more important, we buy the goods and services their networks and outlets endlessly advertise. The stakeholders of top-down government are committed to representing us but asking for little else—except our opinions, our votes, and, of course, our dollars in the form of consumption, contributions, or taxes. They are not aliens from another planet, are no better or worse than the rest of us, and goodness knows they mean to serve our interests, too. If they cannot offer solutions for our social problems, they, at least, consider what placebos might help, placebos being promises that "I will please you." Commissions are appointed, studies are made, reports are issued, bills are introduced, and, of course, there are the attendant speeches and campaigns as the churning goes on. I use the term "churning" because most politicians and their professional advisers are rarely candid with us about the limits of what they can accomplish on our behalf. Have we put too many of our eggs in their basket?

The media pigeonholes us into two convenient stereotypes—consumer and voter. Such media sorting, however, is not a sufficient description of the multifaceted roles that we play and can play in the public world. How things happen in that world is a more complicated story and not the story usually told by those of the in-charge world or by the talking heads who think that's where the action is. Relying on the central role of top-down government has become the default mode for many couch potato citizens with their participation not even an afterthought. It is far easier for them to entertain themselves with political issues ever present inside the Beltway than trying to make sense of their complicated, interacting, ever-changing public world where there is no apparent design or designer and no central vantage point from which someone can chart, much less control, the process. Like it or not, there is no yellow brick road leading any of us to an Emerald City and certainly no wizard there for us to consult. Our social problems are back home in Kansas.

There is an important distinction between social problems and political issues. Social problems are what we encounter in our everyday lives. Political issues are what we hear and read about. They are framed by politicians, editorial writers, and media commentators, and most everyone likes to argue with family members, friends, and coworkers about who is up, who is down, and blah, blah, blah. There is no end to the merry-go-round and the kibitzing about "Did you catch that interview?" or "Don't you just love his tirades?"[2] The habits of couch potato citizens are partly acquired from an incessant rooting for this sports team or that one, making some think that politics is just another game in which they can indulge the habit of dividing the public world into winners and losers. I'm a diehard fan of the New York Yankees, ready to watch and cheer them on, but their world is far removed from our messy public world which does not have a playbook, timeouts, or the simple frame of rules and playoffs. We are not silly to immerse ourselves in the sports worlds of our choice, but we are silly when we thoughtlessly apply such couch potato habits to the immensely complicated playing fields of our local, state, and federal precincts. There is far too much talk about political issues and far too little attention paid to the social problems we encounter in our everyday lives.

For couch potato citizens, their naïveté or cynicism about government comes, in part, from a mistaken belief that they are relatively powerless. Nonsense! That is, *if* they can put aside some of the distractions now consuming too much of their free time. Think of it—TV, the Internet, home video games. Worthwhile, most would say, but at what expense? It is one big reason that we seem to have less time for public life. Market forces have created an entertainment and sports culture that keeps our free time more than occupied. Americans watch on average five hours of TV per day. The market forces that feed this shabby giant of news, sports, reality shows—you name it—primarily seek only their own profit, not our edification. Even the weather is often presented as some kind of calamitous event. Let it rain or snow and it's labeled a storm. Reporters go out and stand in its windy, wet center with the "fanfare and bravado usually reserved for correspondents in a combat zone."[3] The vast reach of our communication options puts us more in touch with one another, but it also permits us to indulge in the sheer consumption of someone else's opinions, programming, or sales. It may partially explain why some of us are too busy for public life and take the easy way out with a shrug by saying, "It's way beyond me!"

Years ago, C. Wright Mills described Americans as "not radical, not liberal, not conservative, not reactionary; they are inactionary; they are out of it."[4] I think he was wrong then, but in these times, with too many couch potato citizens, I'm not so sure. Besides raising kids, holding down jobs, and commuting to and fro, what time they have favors TV and computer screens. Consequently, the consumption of entertainment not only competes with but seems to prevail over associational life and public life in general. Who thinks of joining friends, neighbors, co-workers in trying to help school dropouts get back to school, by engaging the elderly as they cope with their aging and other health issues, or by trying to find ways of sharing more of what we have with those who have far less? Limited time is not the problem. The problem is our perception of how we should use our discretionary time. We are no longer so much a "people" as we are an "audience."

For a moment, however, imagine a loss of electric power that shuts off much of our media. What would we do? We'd look out the window or call friends to see how many others have been affected. We might even get up and out and commiserate with others, friend and stranger alike, who are also deprived. Then imagine how we might organize to cope together at least until power returns. What at first was a personal crisis becomes a collective crisis that prompts us and others to find ways to manage. No one, of course, would wish for such a crisis, but I sketch it here to show how many new relationships might arise, how many new coping mechanisms might be generated if circumstances drove us out of our entertainment ruts into the public world where we shared the outage problem with all those similarly situated. There we will find long-standing social problems just outside or down the street, across town, and across the country that need our attention. And we just might find them sooner if for a moment the media's ever present landscape of entertainment was removed from our sight and we were forced to see other folks and their problems, or perhaps to share our problems with them.

Robert Bellah got it right when he said, "A good society is one in which attention takes precedence over distraction."[5] In such a world, what I call "social attention" directed at social problems of our own making, means self-organizing—an old American habit with new promise at a time when governments, at every level, lack the resources or political will to stand in for us. Our social attention and self-organizing can help us explore different ways of banding together, where everyone counts, to do what government cannot or should not do for us, or more precisely, what government cannot do for us without us—promoting health care beyond the doctor's office, educating young people beyond the school zone, and pooling our resources to help those in greatest need. There is a whole public world out there, a self-organizing world we necessarily share with others, a world beyond government coercion or market incentives as young and old line up at a wellness festival downtown to get free screening for cholesterol levels, skin analysis, and hearing tests; as others crowd source about their health, adding to a growing database for various diseases; as members of the Tohono O'odham community in Arizona offer traditional foods to hospitals, schools, and elderly lunch programs to reduce an astronomical rate of adult diabetes; as local residents pack up Yankee Stadium's prepared but unserved food after a day game and transport it to seniors, kids, and anyone else needing a good meal. Whatever the social problem, the solutions won't come from just more litigation, more legislation, more regulation, or more funding. Real social change is more complicated than that. Simply put, government did not create our social problems nor will it solve them for us. They require *our* social attention.

My focus here is on three important social problems—health care, education, and poverty—but there are many, many other problems—family decline, racism, abortion, drug abuse, illegal immigration, scarcity of water resources, abuse of the environment, and on and on.[6] I want to make our often hidden but potentially powerful presence in the public world, the world we necessarily share with others, more prominent. What many of us keep missing is that many of the social problems we see are of our own making. Obesity is visible everywhere you look. You often see teens hanging out when you know classes in the high school are still in session. A homeless woman asks you for whatever you can spare. These are social problems, not just political issues, and given the financial swoon of 2008 and its aftermath, hard-pressed governments—local, state, or federal—have fewer resources, financial or otherwise, to compensate for our failure to do something about them. With government spending in retreat, plain and simple, we are more indispensable than ever. No, not because we are so wise and virtuous, but indispensable if we really want to get something done. I am one of those who sides with the wisdom of crowds point of view in which "better solutions" can emerge from our bottom-up self-organizing than what "any group of Platonic guardians could come up with"[7]—something of our own making.

We live in a transitional period in which centralized thinking is inadequate without decentralized action—a shift perhaps from government to governance where everyone counts. Yes, I know there are those who think "the people" has always been an overstated and romantic vision of a collective potential never realized. I don't go down that populist road. Instead, I recall in chapter 2 how many social initiatives have been our doing, not the government's, episodes in our history when citizen participation was the seed, the growth, and the decisive measure in successfully addressing seemingly intractable social problems. In a nation where the founders did not think of structuring citizen participation so much as curbing the capacity of the state, our social attention and self-organizing have been all the more remarkable when we found enough others to advance workers' rights or civil liberties or gender equality. Those in charge eventually responded, and what they did was important too, but the story was not about them.

When I say everyone counts, I mean for better or worse—that is what each of us does or does not do. After all, that is what democracy is about—a "process" to be engaged, not a "product" for which we try to hold others accountable.[8] So many find fault with government because they really believe there are solutions and they think government fails to find them. "There is no fixed environment," however "detached from and external to" us.[9] We may act as if such a world exists beyond our making but it doesn't. Our perception of who has power can intimidate us or embolden us. The critical part is how accurate our perception is. If we leave ourselves out, then we are little more than passive spectators instead of active players. Such a sour grapes attitude is easy enough to develop when too many think that what they can't have, they don't want. But like the fox who spurned the grapes that seemed out of reach, we should not dismiss what we would gladly have. Instead, we should think more and do more to bring what we would gladly have within our reach. Like it or not, our *coordination* and *adaptation*, contingent behavior that is driven, in part, by what others do, account for the *emergence* of most social outcomes both good and bad—outcomes that are often not intended on anyone's part. They are our "invisible hand" in a public world, the world we necessarily share with others, where no one's in charge.

Social problem solving, however, requires far more than the everyday outcomes we typically produce. To rework an insight of Parker Palmer, the problem-solving answers we seek in a decentralized world are not "out there" where we think power and expertise reside, nor are they "in here" where each individual resides—the answers lie "between us."[10] That is why I take a fresh look at some of the enduring or evolving social structures, what I call scaffoldings, that can help us find enough others and realize our collective potential for social problem solving. These scaffoldings include our *networks* that technology now connects so effortlessly, our *memberships* that develop loyalties and make us more willing to do our part, and our *public spaces* that help bring us together. Such scaffoldings are especially appropriate in this decentralized era when so many of us work and live in impersonal settings—scaffoldings serve as platforms in the absence of tight knit communities and neighborhoods. Scaffoldings are not what we ultimately build but what we need to stand on in order to build.

My mother-in-law, now deceased, loved doing jigsaw puzzles, and she was quite good at it. She did, however, have the box cover with a picture as guide and goal for her assembly of the pieces. Unfortunately, neither government nor the rest of us have such help for social problem solving in a decentralized world. Public institutions, like private organizations, confront a quandary perhaps best summarized by the oft-used example: "If only HP [its executives] knew what HP [its employees] knows," which means that everyone has something to contribute, not just those supposedly in charge. In a decentralized era, it should be obvious that social problem solving is far more than regulation, or legislation, or more funding. Social problem solving also requires that enough of us change habits that may contribute to social problems and take up new social practices instead. When democracy is at work, it has no centralized mind-set. I don't deny the existence of constitutional and statutory power as vested in elected and appointed officials, but those in charge are not necessarily productive on our behalf unless we join them in social problem solving. The collapse of the overcentralized Soviet system makes that point emphatically. The fiscal dilemmas now facing our governments are reason enough to doubt their capacities.

In a decentralized world it is really not a them-or-us proposition but a challenge of using all the jigsaw pieces we have. It is not that we are all equal in capacity and influence but only that we are all needed. It is not that all of our mutual undertakings will be cooperative. They indeed sometimes may be adversarial, but that they will be more legitimate and likely of more success than when those in charge try to make some progress without us. Think about it for a moment. Most new social practices have started with the social attention and self-organizing of private citizens joining together in the public world to right some wrong, to bring about some change, or to defend something worth defending. And now, given the current bleak economic picture, social attention and self-organizing offer the promise of being both cheaper and more effective than anything government alone can do. I am a pragmatist at heart, and I think what has worked for us should be renewed and built on. E. B. White once remarked that he arose in the morning torn between a desire to improve the world and a desire to enjoy it, and that made it hard to plan the day.[11] I happen to believe that what White described is a pleasant dilemma for all of us and an unavoidable one for men and women in a free society who consider themselves still capable of self-governing.

Of course, one can become the captive of a particular point of view, ignoring counterfactuals and seeing most everything through the lens of one's own making. So I run the risk of failing to acknowledge what others see. I invite you to correct my vision where you think yours can help. I'm not trying here to override the obvious limitations of our human nature, but I am arguing that within those limitations we are capable of doing far more about our social problems than we may think we can and certainly more than we are currently doing.

My aim in writing the book is not to solve our social problems but to show how social problems can be solved, or more accurately how social problems might be ameliorated. Maybe it will take a culture change, both complicated and prolonged, but I agree with Richard Rorty that you have to describe the country not only "in terms of what you know it to be now" but also "in terms of what you passionately hope it will become."[12] Whether it becomes a better country or just a different country remains to be seen. Listen. Can you hear it? Like the sound of a marching band far down the road, the music of our public world on the move again. Listen, it's getting closer. There, can you see it? The parade comes into sight. We are the ones we've been waiting for.

Chapter 1: Government Is Not the Problem or the Solution

The chapter looks at the stakeholders of top-down government, particularly inside the Beltway, and why too many of us expect too much of government when it comes to solving our social problems. Some wrongly assume that those ostensibly in charge know what they're doing from the outset. I offer less flattering explanations, which I think more accurately account for what really goes on in their stakeholder world. Most people don't know, and by getting the story straight, we can better understand why that world can't fix social problems without us. Storytelling in government is less an art than a series of accidents, and how things happen is certainly a more complicated story than the cartoon portrayals that the media often indulges in.

The chapter also looks at Obama's Organizing for America, which did little to retool its successful campaign operation. Instead of getting Obama's supporters engaged in their communities, OFA used this remarkable network of citizens as essentially a lobbying arm to get top-down legislation moving inside the Beltway. Organizing for America seems, too often, to be organizing for Obama—a necessary campaign dynamic but far from a culture change. I also examine the understandable but flawed assumption that letting the private sector do whatever needs doing is preferable to leaving government to do it. From my experience, business does what is doable and profitable, with government getting all the rest.

Chapter 2: It's Us . . .

So if the stakeholders of top-down government can't begin to solve our social problems or can't afford to even try any longer, guess what? It's us . . . we are the ones we've been waiting for. What better time to recall America's never-ending story of social attention and self-organizing to solve social problems? The chapter will offer numerous examples from everyday life to show how the actions of countless people have accounted for the bottom-up origins of countless good outcomes—libraries and blood banks, sanctuaries and land trusts, hospice teams and day care centers, crime watches and welcome wagons, search parties and self-help groups, and on and on. What many keep missing is that the outcomes they see have often been the work of their neighbors, friends, and ordinary citizens just like them.

The chapter also looks at the necessary politics of social problem solving complicated by the current hang-up of too many citizens ceding far too much problem-solving authority to those with professional credentials. The chapter concludes by recounting episodes when the dynamic of self-organizing scaled up to social movements which changed dramatically our country's status quo—workers' rights, civil rights, and gender equality—a story of brotherhoods, sisterhoods, churches, and diverse private associations far removed from the nation-state.

Chapter 3: . . . And Enough Others

The chapter examines the obvious challenge of finding *enough others* to make bottom-up change more than just a topic for blog talk. After all, some things worth doing are just not worth doing unless we can find enough others to join in. Then I offer a few caveats about the role of local, regional, and nationwide NGOs whose agendas also address social problems. Such reservations lead me to identify other scaffoldings that may help us find *enough others* including informal *social networks*, local club and church *memberships*, and *public spaces*. Are the social scaffoldings we now have sturdy enough to promote new social practices which can scale up to make a real difference? I look at each such scaffolding.

The chapter then looks at the familiar excuses of couch potato citizens: "I don't know enough," or "I can't make a difference," or "I've got better things to do." There are no ready answers for these obstacles, and far be it from me to make things simple when the heart of my argument says they are not, but I do offer a closer look at the likely degrees of cooperation of those who may be drawn to any particular undertaking. Then the discussion moves to the incentives or stratagems that can be used to keep as many engaged as possible.

Chapter 4: And Here Come the Boomers

Some say that real social change comes only with crisis. Certainly those in government see the aging of the Boomer generation as a looming crisis of how to pay their Social Security entitlements and Medicare costs down the road. This chapter sees such a crisis in a different way. My argument is that these same Boomers, more than 75 million of them, are fast approaching the time—the first wave reached 65 in 2011—when they are likely to develop, by choice or circumstance, new social practices for their own sake as well as for the sake of others. Call it a crisis of aging, but it is also an opportunity to break new ground. Many Boomers may discover that they have more time to devote to social problems like our making excessive demands of the health care system, failing to adequately educate young people, or consuming more than anyone should while others go without.

There are certainly enough Boomers, *enough others*, to make a substantial contribution in dealing with such problems. So the concern of the chapter is not what government is going to do about the Boomers but what the Boomers have the potential of doing—pursuing health care beyond the doctor's office, educating young people beyond the school zone, and pooling their abundant resources in new ways—given what they own, what they know, and what free time they may have.

Chapter 5: One Thing Can Lead to Another

Assuming new social practices take root and the Boomers can help make it so, one thing can lead to another. I can imagine government's support for emerging social practices as likely to be far more productive than just trying to pay the bills for health care, education, and welfare. I can imagine some professionals on call, including pollsters and experts, responding to our social attention and the self-organizing example we set by deliberating with us as equals. More pollsters could pursue the give and take of deliberation with us rather than just doing more statistical sampling and choosing what polling topics to put before us. More experts on call could be open to thinking *with* us rather than *for* us. I can also imagine new forms of online coverage making the news of what we are doing to secure new social practices.

Finally the chapter asks readers where they think we should direct our social attention. What social practices would they like to see emerge and scale up? Such questions are meant to tap their experience and stimulate their imagination so they can take the book's argument in directions which they care most about. *The Real Change-Makers* can then become not just a good read but a tool for change. After all, one thing can lead to another.

CHAPTER 1

Government Is Not the
Problem or the Solution

"Making believe!" cried Dorothy. "Are you not a great Wizard?"

"Hush, my dear," he said; "don't speak so loud. Or you will
be overheard—and I should be ruined. I'm supposed to be a great
Wizard."

"And aren't you?" she asked.

"Not a bit of it, my dear; I'm just a common man."

The Wizard of Oz, by L. Frank Baum

This chapter focuses on the stakeholders of top-down government—
politicians, professionals on call, the 24/7 media—and the storytelling they all indulge in. Such folks populate or circle around top-down
government—the place too many people assume is the center of action
for doing something about our social problems. So top-down government gets heaping helpings of all kinds of social problems, many of
which couch potato citizens think are beyond their reach. They are not,
in fact, if we give them our social attention instead of just clogging the
arteries of governments already contending with fiscal deficits and budget crises, which may weigh them down for years to come. Some of us
fool ourselves, as do many stakeholders, that school dropouts, obese
neighbors, and the homeless on the street are problems that someone
at some level of government can take care of. Not true. Until we reconsider our attitudes about how such problems arise and how we should
address them, we really have little chance, as does government itself, to
do much about them.[1]

These days plenty of citizens want to shrink the federal government. They sign petitions or join protest rallies, but fail to actually practice what they preach—how to get government off their backs. How, indeed, when it is they who ride that beast, not the other way around. They want to reduce the federal deficit but don't touch Medicare, don't touch Social Security, and lower their taxes, please. They rarely consider what *they* might do to reduce soaring health costs. They go to a school board meeting to protest funding for more special education programs but fail to see what they might do to get their children to spend more time reading and writing. They object to government spending on the poor but rarely lift a finger to share the surplus of their local resources with those in need. They ignore the fact that the who and how of social change starts with all of us doing more if they want government doing less. Think back to when cigarette smoking was rampant among us even when mounting evidence told us that it was a killer habit. Then, from the bottom up, social attention took aim at those who smoked in workspaces and public spaces and government did its part by curbing, taxing, and otherwise discouraging the habit. My disapproving daughter practically ran me out of the house any time I lit up an after-dinner cigar. Later, the folks next door in our apartment building asked me to cease and desist as they could detect my habit on their side of the common walls we shared. It had become their social problem and I had to do something about it. No one can tell me that government forced my hand. Family members and neighbors did. Like it or not, social problems often come close to home—young people dropping out of school, families eating cheap food and becoming obese together, the homeless seeking refuge in public places—problems that are visible whether or not we give them adequate social attention. Such problems, sooner or later, land at the doorstep of top-down government but their origins are our doing, or our neighbors' doing, or the doing of those across town we may not know but encounter at the public intersections of our daily lives.

It's only natural to look to representative government for help. It is, in part, our creation and servant so you will not find me part of the current rant of those who treat government as if it were an enemy rather than the ally it is meant to be. I spent enough years in government, at federal, state, and local levels, to know that decent, well-meaning Americans go to work there every day trying to make it work on our behalf. Their performance is no better, but certainly no worse, than the performance of those in the for-profit and nonprofit sectors—sectors which I also spent time working in and learning about. When I say "government is not the problem," I don't mean to imply that its performance is unassailable. Far from it, but we should not think that it is our primary option for doing something about our social problems. Too many of us expect too much of the stakeholders of top-down government when it comes to actually getting much done about such problems. And some of the problem-churning inside the Beltway is partly our own doing. At various times, we have mobilized through social movements and special-interest lobbying to address one social problem or another, racial discrimination, age discrimination, gender discrimination, endangerment of species, and so many others. As rights and entitlements have been secured, it's fair to say that national standards have often proven to be a two-edged sword. The understandable pursuit of justice for every individual often ignores the social linkages that promote a different kind of ideal—social attention to others' needs without law or regulation to facilitate such attention. For example, some have used affirmative action as a blunt instrument with little local attention—tutoring and mentoring—for disadvantaged students or job seekers. As a consequence, the habit of pursuing legal remedies beyond the communities we live in has made finding social remedies within our communities less likely with the idea of community itself being breached. And it has put government at a greater distance from John Stuart Mill's 19th-century conception of the state:

> What the state can usefully do is to make itself a central depository, and active circulator and diffuser, of the experience resulting from many trials. Its business is to enable each experimentalist to benefit by the experiments of others: instead of tolerating no experiments but its own.[2]

Very few these days, however, entertain the romantic notion that we can somehow get along without the beast inside the Beltway. Most of us long ago became willing prisoners of its embrace and power to conduct foreign wars and collect and spend tax revenues supposedly on our behalf. It is, in part, an understandable but unexamined reflex we have developed for seeking protective measures that promote security and order. The threat of corrupt financial practices and terrorist networks are just two examples of our need for centralized measures to protect us. Unfortunately, there has been an added twist in what is thought of as representative government. We have been typecast as customers, not as citizens. The reinventing government initiative of the Clinton administration, led by Vice President Al Gore, left the impression that we are not the ultimate owners of government but merely a market for its services. And President Bush, in the aftermath of September 11, told us that we could play a constructive role by getting out and going shopping. Think of what that said about us. We are seen primarily as consumers in the eyes of too many of the stakeholders of top-down government. What a dreary prospect!

Politicians and Professionals On Call

From my government experience, I learned that politicians with their professional retinues are over their heads and far from shore. Although the media tags many of our elected representatives as professional politicians, it does not mean they are any better at what they do than their amateur predecessors. What it means is that elective office has become a full-time job and career, which leaves more time for them to play a more central role, along with professionals on call, in trying to do more to solve *our* social problems. And I should not leave out special interest advocates who are often part of the mix too. Parenthetically, let me say that I don't consider "special interests" a dirty word. It was made so when trying to tar those in labor unions in the early 1980s whose influence has recently come under fresh attack.[3] Now, of course, anyone and everyone uses "special interest" pejoratively as if democratic government has not always entertained, and necessarily so, a wide range of "interests" special only because they have specific, self-interested goals. Special interests are not just business and labor lobbyists jostling for attention and influence. They include every organized group seeking to use government to advance its agenda.[4] (Try telling your children next time that in their pleadings for more allowance or later bedtimes they are just "special interests" you can ignore.) That is not to say that special interests are harmless do-gooders. We often end up paying for many of the deals they make with politicians and bureaucrats. It may be democracy at work but it's also a case of small organized groups wagging the tail of the national dog with the costs falling disproportionately on the unorganized.[5] Consequently, so much of the ill will toward government springs from resentment that the highly organized are getting "theirs" at "our" expense.

Look inside the Beltway and you will also find a multitude of professionals on staff or in think tanks and policy associations offering their views and proposals to legislators and administrators—an insider, policy-analysis game that we don't so much watch as hear about after the fact. Even those appointed to blue-ribbon commissions, who ostensibly represent our interests from time to time, usually maintain some distance from those of us outside the Beltway. Professionals on call now dominate the social problem-solving landscape wherever governments reside. Citizens are often just an afterthought. Their policy-analysis game is not child's play, but I like to use the playful analogy of what a group of such professionals might do when trying to decide where to eat together for dinner. Serious analysis would only start when they agreed on what criteria to use for choosing a restaurant (price, décor, service, proximity, etc.) and what restaurant alternatives were available to them within an agreed area or neighborhood. The group would then check out all such restaurants before choosing the one that best met their criteria. Given their exhaustive analysis, however, I would guess the restaurant of their choice would probably be closed for the night before they could get there to eat. It's one reason why oftentimes it takes government so long to get so little done.

With the deep pocket of government and the many entrepreneur politicians that populate it, pollsters are also professionals on call. They always stand ready to take the pulse of a distracted public and to offer advice to whoever will pay for it. Nothing wrong with that, we all have to make a living, but there is little attention paid by this professional cadre to what we do or don't do in our everyday lives. Those who argue that elected officials and policymakers are out of touch with various publics get it all wrong. On the contrary, our opinions and preferences are well documented for them by pollsters, but our potential role in finding new ways to deal with social problems is mostly ignored with pollsters using closed-end questions and providing a list of answer choices, four or five at most. Their polling questions shape our answers. Pollsters see us and our social problems as aggregates, quantifying what they find and organizing their data as if a still picture of public opinion taken on such and such a date can anywhere near reflect the ebb and flow of our individual lives as we are continually buffeted by changing circumstances.

Most professionals on call gravitate to top-down government because the light is better there with what they consider reliable data on which they pile new reports, graphs, and more and more data.[6] They assume that problem solving is government's job and so they stand ready to offer their never-ending briefings for elected and appointed officials. Like magicians, their PowerPoint presentations are interspersed with

"I shall now . . ." or "later I will show," constantly attending to and feeding the ignorance of decision makers in the room.[7] Unfortunately, those with one expertise or another tame what to them is an unmanageable number of variables only to distort how social problems can be addressed. They often give undue weight to those variables they can quantify and incorrectly mistake numbers for cold, hard fact.[8] Furthermore, they like to bend problems to fit within their particular expertise and they often ignore those parts that lie beyond their training and experience. With such a reductionist approach, they prefer to draw a straight line from problem to answer. It's easy enough to draw that line in a PowerPoint presentation but awfully hard to follow it in the real world when so many players, events, and unpredictable happenings push the answer off course. Modeling an answer is like cartooning.[9] It may capture the essence of what society needs but will likely remain elusive when anyone experiences the actual zigzag path that an answer encounters in the real world. Their answers are also driven by *assumptions* largely shaped by their disciplinary training, although such assumptions are rarely acknowledged or examined except within the closed precincts of their respective professional guilds. If, however, the assumptions are wrong, then their answers are likely to be too. Alfred North Whitehead perhaps best described the limitations of professional thinking as "the restraint of serious thought within a groove . . . with the imperfect categories of thought derived from one profession."[10]

The preference of those in top-down government for the supposed solutions of experts is not a new situation. It's been going on for more than a century as progressive thought has too often coupled itself with professional expertise resulting in the exclusion of almost everyone else. Alexis de Tocqueville long ago foresaw this kind of administrative despotism. "It doesn't break men's will but softens, bends, and subdues it; it seldom enjoins, but often inhibits, action; it does not destroy anything but prevents much from being born."[11] It has not been a conspiracy or bad in and of itself; it is the consequences that flow from such professional ascendance that jeopardize a flourishing, shared public life. Those with a professional mind-set surely intend to represent our interests, but there's a twist. How can they represent us if they think they know better than we do how to solve our social problems?[12] The current culture of professionalism rejects inherited class, replacing it with a different kind of class—those who have credentials. And so deference is paid to those whose specialty is beyond our knowing—"I'm not a health economist so I don't have the answer." Yet Charles Lindblom and David K. Cohen advanced the argument that, when it comes to social problem solving, the professional mind-set will always depend heavily on ordinary knowledge, something accessible to everyone. They argued that the academic world, which spawns all manner of professional specialists, fails to understand, or at least to concede, that "a great deal of the world's problem-solving is and ought to be accomplished through various forms of interaction that substitute for thought, understanding, or analysis." Lindblom and Cohen criticized the failure of researchers to disclose that, despite their "specialized investigative techniques, especially quantitative," most of them "inevitably rely heavily on the same ordinary techniques of speculation, definition, conceptualization, hypothesis, formulation, and verification" as are practiced by ordinary citizens.[13]

Nonetheless, too many of us have concluded that we have little to offer and thus little to do about social problems close at hand. We have developed an inferiority complex about our collective potential to fix such social problems ourselves. Our ignorance makes us dote on professionals on call as if they can somehow do our thinking for us about the social problems we share.[14] And our dependence doesn't stop there; we often let expert opinion shape how we should proceed with our spouses, children, and workplace relations. We can be consumed by whatever somebody who knows more, who knows better, tells us. In so doing, we have become entangled in the culture of professionalism blown hither and yon by the opinions of those whom the media anoints as "pundits" for our ready consumption. We yield to those with professional mind-sets granting to them wisdom and power that we deny to ourselves.[15] Our elected officials also like to play it safe making them too willing to follow the advice of those who supposedly know more. In an early draft of a book that I was editing, Harry Boyte eloquently described the damage done by a misshapen form of politics, what he calls "technocratic politics," which for Boyte is "the pattern of domination by experts who are removed from common civic life." Boyte sees "technocratic politics" as spreading "throughout contemporary society like a silent disease. It is largely politics without a name, presenting itself as an objective set of truths, practices, and procedures."[16]

We would like to think that those with supposed power, and those who advise them, can shape outcomes to fit their intentions and that they act intentionally with some end in mind. There are no government decision makers, however, or experts, for that matter, who have calculating minds equal to the complex, rapidly changing environments in which they must operate or analyze. The Bush administration's fearless resolve in 2003 to invade Iraq was certainly scary since there was no possible way that they could foresee the range of consequences of such a decision. They obviously feigned no modesty about U.S. military power, but they had every reason to be more modest about the reliability of their regime-changing scenarios. There were just too many variables for them to account for or control. Those in government who assume they have enough control over events to produce the outcome that they want, despite evidence that they do not, are what I would call "control freaks," whose temperament and professional credentials combine to make them think that they can somehow get a decision dead-on from the outset. Perhaps they have been misled by too many accounts of important discoveries and accomplishments that leave out the drift, procrastination, mistakes, and dumb luck that happened along the way. Confident of their own powers and prospects, they believe they can master any given situation if they have enough time, information, and shrewd foresight. Certainly, rational models of policy analysis and decision making, which professionals on call are usually well-schooled on, encourages such hubris by assuming that a decision maker in sufficient control with a clear objective can choose an alternative that best satisfies that objective and can then proceed to implement it. The Achilles' heel of this "best and brightest" cohort is the intellectual conceit that such close-ordered thinking can produce the outcome they most prefer, but what could be more irrational than trusting that such a linear sequence of thought and planning had sufficient predictive value in the Middle East? How could anyone have known what would happen given the number of stakeholders both in and outside of Iraq reacting to a U.S.-led invasion? The scenario that the Bush administration relied on was just not their story alone to tell.

A real disconnect also exists between the linear paths projected by those in top-down government and the many roads of social attention and citizen action encountered in the real world. Such roads do not take anyone to a single destination but to many different places, and they are rarely reached by following the road maps projected by experts. Social attention to social problems provides no easy or obvious answers. It is the worst kind of reductionism to think otherwise. Neither politics or social problem solving, and they share a lot in common, follow a linear path. I learned from my days in top-down government that it is better to try many pathways that often begin in neighborhoods or among small groups where their work becomes emulated as it develops and succeeds. When New York City's need to curb water consumption produced a government plan for metering homes and apartment buildings, officials discovered that there was no fair scheme for allocating water use within multifamily buildings where 70 percent of city residents then lived. Metering individual apartments was very expensive and very difficult logistically. Without a way to meter each apartment, a building would have to pay for its total use. But who would pay? If a building had a lot of large or doubled-up families, or if tenants were home all day using water, some people would pay a disproportionate amount for others' use. Furthermore, if the landlord could not pass on the cost, building abandonments were a serious risk. So even with government intervention, the water conservation plan ended up depending on millions of New Yorkers voluntarily changing their individual behavior. Soon the city's Department of Environmental Conservation ran full-page ads encouraging New Yorkers to turn off the tap when brushing their teeth, to use washers and dishwashers only with full loads, and to limit showers to three minutes.[17]

Too many professional politicians and experts fail to realize that the professional orientation of proposing a solution for what they think we need, instead of including us to determine together what is desirable or actually possible, is no solution at all. So when expert opinions clash, and they often do, someone must be wrong.[18] More important, it opens up a wide swath of social problem solving to those of us who do not know who to believe. Instead of just relying on experts' judgments, we have our own judgments and access to the collective judgment of neighbors, friends, and coworkers. It's not a matter of who is right, expert or not; it's who is needed to get something done about a social problem, and that's us. To build a public life involves more than just making room for those without professional credentials. The current culture of professionalism has to somehow change, which means finding ways of learning from those who have credentials, and they from us, in open forums where we can deliberate together as equals about our common problems and possibilities; I explore this further in chapter 5.

The 24/7 Media and Storytelling in Government

An obvious stakeholder of top-down government is the 24/7 news media. For them, it's a lot cheaper to cover the news inside the Beltway than try to cover what's happening locally across the country. Besides, there is substantial media competition to satisfy the daily appetites of couch potato citizens for what's going on inside the Beltway. It doesn't make any difference which side of the couch citizens sit on, left or right; they are avid consumers of the partisan combat that lights up their screens. But demand exceeds supply and so, to make up the difference, there is an enormous market for junk news. Like junk food, its packaging is attractive but its content has next to no value. The 24/7 news media presents a full helping of unexamined headlines and gratuitous commentary. The format provides little time for thoughtful analysis and most of the commentary consists of crude verbal combat between talking heads who are there more to entertain than to enlighten. There is much doting on personalities, not just about top-down politicians but among the news teams themselves. Only the news can be ugly but never the anchors themselves. Ratings and profits come first with news judgment and responsible journalism lagging far behind.

A TV reporter once told me that the 24/7 news media is "giving people what they want." It was an understandable choice of words for a medium that justifies almost everything it puts on the air by the same yardstick. Some viewers are undoubtedly interested in substance, but with so many channels offering so little, it keeps them busy flicking their remotes looking for some nourishment. The banalities of junk news can starve them with mindless advocacy, not thoughtful analysis. The preference for politics as a form of combat far overshadows politics as a form of problem solving. What the media delivers in a 24-hour news cycle demands an enormous amount of chatter and winging it to fill the time. I don't think that such shows can be dismissed as harmless entertainment when their junk news is sold to such a vast audience day after day, night after night, reinforcing the habit of couch potato citizens as being little more than junk consumers. What is so sad is that such vacuous and cynical news presentation too often demeans government for whatever it tries to do without ever thinking to challenge couch potato citizens to get up and do something themselves. Instead of being the midwife of those who would labor to make self-government succeed, the 24/7 media throws its lot in with the stakeholders of top-down government despite playing its adversary role. Alex Jones has rightly noted that much of the media is moving from "news of verification" to "news of assertion," which dominates much of the prime time on cable news channels.[19] The media does not go so far as to tell us what to think, but it does wave its arms and jumps up and down as it tells us what to think *about*.

The 24/7 media needs experts, too, to provide some ballast to its otherwise gratuitous commentaries. What do anchors know that some expert knows better? So put him on, or let her opine, for a credentials-soaked audience. Some experts thrive on the media if they can deliver simple, decisive statements that are easier to package in sound bites. Listen to one candid, but unnamed, "expert": "I fight to preserve my reputation in a cutthroat adversarial culture. I woo dumb-ass reporters who want glib sound bites."[20] Although an expert would be embarrassed to sound so simple-minded in the company of his professional peers, the media doesn't have time for too many qualifying statements or "on the one hand and on the other" kind of talk. The media favors experts who put aside subtleties and equivocation for the projection of a forceful personality full of opinion allowed to pass for fact. As a result, the media demeans both the expert and its audience by dumbing down the conversation. Media credibility is not so much earned as delegated to any expert who has the talent to keep it short before the program goes on to its next commercial.[21]

Let me move from the presentation of news to the news itself—junk or not. News is not what happened but a story about what supposedly happened, and that brings me to the significance of storytelling in government.[22] When my work was in the public eye, I was struck with how often news stories—and that's what we call them, "stories"—constructed accounts about what top-down government was doing that didn't correspond to what I knew was going on.[23] If you have ever sat on a jury you probably have experienced firsthand how storytelling becomes a shared enterprise as you, along with others in the jury room, try to make sense of what happened from the testimony presented in court. Jury members can become the authors, not just the readers of what happened. We are certainly influenced by what others think happened—the story is not so much discovered as developed by our jury deliberations. Reporters also organize the facts in a sequence that seems plausible including their guesswork about who intended what. Storytelling imputes intention after the fact, even if there was, in fact, no intention. Sometimes I would read stories about what the mayor or the governor or some department head intended, when I knew of no such intent at all. What we call "spin makers" in government further distort reported events. They don't tell it like it is, but tell it like they want others to believe it is. The very human need for making sense of a jumble of events accounts for the storytelling that goes on, not just by the media, but by a bewildered president, governor, or mayor, who often find it hard to fathom the beast they ride. Since the electoral success of a new CEO is in large part due to the voters' approval of what he or she has vowed to do, little notice is taken as to whether he or she knows how to do it. Every candidate plans how to win. Virtually no candidate plans how to manage change in the event of victory. He is now the president, she is now the governor, he is now the mayor—a majority of voters have called their bluff.

Storytelling entertains but often does little to educate us about how government actually works in a complex, public world.[24] I noted in an earlier work of mine that it reminds me of the gyrations of the stock market the financial media try to make sense of by producing their instant storylines about what motivated investors on a given day. The pundits assign a cause for market moves without offering the thousand *other* reasons why buyers and sellers traded shares that day. Likewise, how ready the media is when covering government stories to make sense of what often is inexplicable may be far, far from being sensible. It's only natural to minimize the number of variables to support an assumption that whatever happened has an explanation. They often ignore the messy process, the trial and error that produced an outcome. In storytelling, as common and as necessary as it is, too much is left out and thus we are misled about how things actually happen in government. The common, but carelessly used, term "problem solving" in top-down government usually overstates what actually happens. When they talk about solving a problem what they actually mean is simply improving the situation. Let me repeat: they are over their heads and far from shore. An outcome that emerges may be some distance from the place where they started and may not resemble where they thought they were headed.

Power is in the perception of who we think has power in government. By storytelling, their own or the media's version, those ostensibly in charge acquire a kind of power which creates or confirms our perception of who has it. Decision makers provide highly edited versions of what are often stumbling, mistake-filled journeys. In retelling, the bad parts are usually left out. They try to reconstruct what happened to satisfy themselves that they acted rationally and that their story coheres, or they merely want to make sense of what otherwise would be bewildering to them as well as others.[25] Remember: whoever it is, you, me, or the president of the United States, we each live through a set of experiences without knowing what the outcome will be. Nonetheless, we often subordinate whatever we actually did to fit a storyline that makes sense to others. We provide a sequence, a story *after the fact* that organizes what we would like to think happened—maybe it did, maybe it didn't, but at least we have a story to tell that others can nod their heads to. It's only natural to leave out so much that in retrospect seems beside the point given the outcome that is in hand. And so we say "the bottom line" or "to make a long story short" or "the point I'm trying to make." Perhaps that's all that others want to hear about, but they certainly learn far less about what actually happened. Does it make a difference? I think so when it comes to the who and how of government storytelling. Stories, regardless of what government source they come from, usually leave out the drift of events, procrastination, mistakes, and dumb luck that happen along the way.

Drift is a good way to describe how a public agenda of problems can sometimes get only fitful attention. This is especially true in agencies where the top positions are political appointments and such appointees come and go with some regularity. With little continuity or predictability in how an agenda should be addressed or by whom, problems sometimes wander from one division of an agency to another or from one task force to another looking for attention. If and when a problem finally gets the attention it deserves, the story is not about the wandering path it took.

Then there is *procrastination*. Executives and legislators have limits to what personal capital they are willing to spend on any particular project. Given the rough-and-tumble nature of politics, such capital can be easily wasted and difficult to replenish. Procrastination then conveniently arises when executives and legislators confront undesirable alternatives such as budget cuts or tax hikes. They simply put off action to see what develops. They permit or invite interventions that may somehow take the monkey off their backs. Instead of leading, they hope to follow some deeper pocket or a more secure office holder.

And there are the *mistakes* and there are a-plenty in government—some we hear about, most we do not. A more genteel way of talking about the mistakes that are made is "trial and error," which is true in any trade or profession, but rarely admitted after the fact in government briefings and press conferences.

Dumb luck we almost never hear about, much less is it freely disclosed by those in government. I have told the story before of when I was in City Hall and we negotiated a difficult and expensive labor contract with little public resistance because a citywide newspaper strike meant fewer outlets were available for an editorial and public backlash. For those of us in City Hall, the newspaper strike was a piece of dumb luck in which the story got lost, at least for awhile. Certainly, no one in City Hall made note of it in taking credit for the relative calm in which we got the deal done. I recall other potential news stories that, fortunately, never saw the light of day in press releases, press conferences, or media interviews:

A prominent real estate developer offered the city valuable land at a prime location for a convention center that the city wanted to build. The developer came to me and said that he was willing to forego a $500,000 fee, which the city would be obligated to pay him for his role in the transaction, if the city would name the proposed center after the developer's father—a respectable real estate mogul in his own right.

A police lieutenant called me at midnight to report that a prominent legislator's car had been towed from a "no parking" zone and was being held until the towing charges were paid. The lieutenant said that the legislator was very angry and refused to pay. The lieutenant told me that he had assured the state senator that his car would be released if I gave the OK.

A newspaper's editorial severely criticized police officers threatening to walk off the job if a labor contract was not settled quickly and to their liking. In retaliation, off-duty policemen delayed the newspaper's delivery trucks by blocking their garage exits. The managing editor called me and demanded that all off-duty policemen be disarmed immediately to eliminate any further intimidation of the newspaper's drivers.

Whatever the outcomes in our municipal administration, they were rarely solutions, and the stories rarely finished, given the ceaseless flow of events that made and remade outcomes without end. I found that too many thought that policy was made by a few of us in some inner circle of power. The story was often told that way, but policy was the stuff of many, many players. I remember an assistant secretary of commerce badgering me when I served as deputy mayor for policy about the city being late with an economic development policy report. I took him to a window high up in the World Trade Center that featured a panoramic view of New York City, and pointed out the respective boroughs of the city. "There's Staten Island with the population of Richmond, Virginia. Over there is Brooklyn with as many people as live in L.A." Turning further in our glass perch, I nodded toward the borough of Queens, the size of Philadelphia. "Up there is the Bronx with the population of San Francisco and Boston, and we're standing in Manhattan as large as Detroit." Turning, I smiled and said: "It's a big, complicated place; give us a little more time."[26]

Top-down government is far more than those at the top. But to read their out-of-office lookbacks you would think they always were at the center of any significant problem-solving decision—shaping it, driving it, reconciling others' differences with it. To the victors go the spoils and so, too, those who hold the power get to tell the story, but it's only *their* story, not *the* story, which often includes layer upon layer of legislative staff, administrative departments, advisers, consultants, or lobbyists who could offer their own versions. And then there is the media with their own scoops and headlines but with far less attention to, and follow-up of, the unanswered question: "Then what happened?" It is on that subsequent journey where a story can wander off, or paths get crossed, and the problem solving does not happen. Too rarely, the media pursues such a story and learns that the doing didn't get done and with all good intentions, the shaggy beast got lost somewhere along the way.

Despite the serious limitations of those in public office, many of us would like to think they are up to dealing with our social problems because the stories they tell make some of us believe that they are. Their stories create an impression of knowing more and doing more than they actually know and do.[27] With the media as information and event broker, we rely on their storytelling to help us comprehend how and why certain outcomes emerge. This is all quite understandable, but, unfortunately, the media, as outsiders trying to make sense of what insiders are trying to do, abbreviate and distort how things happen, all of them preferring to tidy up what would be an otherwise partial or even incoherent story. It is understandable that we look for a central cause, whether we think government is doing too much or too little, rather than try to fathom the multitude of influences that account for whatever outcomes emerge in the usually long, unfinished story of social problem solving. Perhaps most of us would like to believe that if we cannot be in control of the outcomes, then someone else is, but it's very hard to imagine or reconstruct the complex processes that contribute to any story of social problem solving. That's why we are all too ready to pin that burden or blame on government rather than see that we are inextricably part of the story too.

Organizing for America (OFA)

It is disappointing that Obama's Organizing for America did so little to retool its successful campaign operation into something more. When Obama entered the presidential primaries in early 2007, some observers characterized his "generational call to arms . . . more as a movement" than just another political campaign.[28] A movement it has not proved to be and one major reason has been how Obama and his people have used it. Instead of getting Obama's supporters engaged in their communities, OFA used this remarkable network of citizens as essentially a lobbying arm to get top-down legislation moving inside the Beltway. OFA was not so much organizing for America as organizing for the Obama administration. One and the same? I don't think so; that leaves too much out and too many Americans. Sad to say, government increasingly mobilizes us when our collective voice is needed, which is very different from our bottom-up history when we originated the action.[29]

Early on when OFA asked me what it should be doing in local communities, I emphasized that each group of community organizers should determine what needed fixing where they worked and lived; that the energy of the '08 Obama campaign needed local nourishment by growing initiatives that addressed local problems. Subsequently, I saw very little evidence that OFA in Washington, DC, thought such bottom-up work was a priority. In fact, at one time OFA reported that 83.9 percent of their mailing list agreed that "helping the president pass legislation through grassroots efforts should be a top goal for OFA." Sixty-three percent, however, thought local issues should also be on OFA's agenda, but going forward they didn't get much OFA attention. Instead, OFA sent a drumbeat of emails urging locals to support whatever timely initiative the Obama administration needed help with inside the Beltway. Locals were asked to visit their senator's office to bring attention to pending legislation on health care. The undertaking was labeled Office Visits for Health Reform. They were asked to tell a personal story and drop off an OFA customized flyer. Then locals were asked to call their respective U.S. House representatives to thank them for already being on board with health care reform. OFA wanted locals to help start a chain letter to friends linking them to the OFA undertaking and to donate $3 or $5 "to lay the groundwork for the fights ahead." Then, David Plouffe, Obama's political captain, asked locals to download OFA's document called "Benefits of Wall Street Reform" and use it as a handout at local coffee shops or grocery stores or take it door-to-door. Locals seemed needed only to help the Obama administration address its agenda. Community initiatives not tied to the national agenda got short shrift. Obama's rhetoric shifted from "we were the change we seek" to we were the locals that the Obama administration needed. Most of OFA's one-way communication for the remainder of the 2009 congressional session stayed focused on health care reform. By OFA's estimate, 1.5 million Americans were involved. OFA held a contest to choose a winning ad as part of OFA's "Health Reform Video Challenge" and asked locals to buy a $25 T-shirt at an OFA online store to pay for OFA's efforts or to make a $3 donation so they could win a chance of a trip to Las Vegas to be at the president's side at a campaign rally. One appeal simply pleaded, "We need to raise $300,000 by Thursday."

Michelle Obama's own efforts came much closer to getting locals involved in their communities as she took on the childhood obesity problem, a "Feed a Neighbor" initiative, and helping families of veterans and active service members in each community. On the Martin Luther King holiday, Michelle encouraged everyone to engage in service to their communities with food drives, neighborhood clean-ups, and in the case of the Obamas, a Boys and Girls Club event. These were not inside the Beltway pleadings but requests for action on all local fronts. Still the great majority of messages out of DC were about helping to make history with little attention to local startups. Preparing for the 2010 midterm elections, OFA options included making sure people registered to vote, writing to the local newspaper, going door to door, and calling potential supporters. OFA was right back to 2008 with lots at stake to be sure but still paying very little attention to grassroots work on anything but the Obama administration's terms. It was not surprising that fatigue set in and active support for the Obama agenda fell off, which probably had some measure of influence on the 2010 midterm election results.

I don't suppose anyone should have expected more from a political campaign morphing into a quasi-government website. It's only that there was an opportunity to do much, much more. The problem with top-down government, whoever are the ones in power, is that the representative role trumps anything else. And as important as that representative agenda is, whatever administration takes charge pays too little attention to the potential of getting social problem solving started from the bottom up. George H. W. Bush often talked about "a thousand points of light"—a useful metaphor for local initiatives, but although it was part of the Bush rhetoric, his administration didn't do much to reconnect Americans to each other and to their communities. The outlook was more libertarian than conservative, a radical individualism that only paid lip service to Edmund Burke's "little platoons"— the local institutions of community life. Bill Clinton also looked at the issue of civic reconnection, but I know from my own experience with his project that very little came of it.[30] Will the same be said for Barack Obama?

Privatization

And then there is the private sector—the place where so many citizens think our problems might be handled more efficiently. Privatization has been mostly defined as "the use of nongovernmental organizations to run government programs." It's not about getting things done without government; it's an emphasis on what some think is better management when in private, business hands. A lot of the support for privatization comes from those who think many problems need the technical fix that the private sector can better provide. But this is where privatization has reinforced top-down government by becoming its agent, so to speak. It was not meant to be a source or example for citizens to emulate. Such thinking sees social problem solving not as a social enterprise but as finding a solution. Democratic process? Citizen input? Just get the problem solved, damn it! Such thinking assumes that someone has the smarts to clear things up, has the expertise to find the technical means of setting things straight. Those with such thinking, impatient couch potato citizens or strident champions of the private sector, just don't see social problem solving from the bottom up as a possible avenue to pursue. Instead, the private sector has the brains, or they make good products, or they provide good service. Surely they can get the job done.

Some of the steam of privatization, however, evaporated after the 2008 financial swoon when many people's confidence and trust in the private sector eroded, to say the least. Nonetheless, privatization is a staple of conservative thought whenever there's talk about what to do about this problem or that and who will do it. Conservatives neglect, however, to note that the public agenda is often shaped by those tasks the private sector either failed or declined to do much about. When government is taken to task, it's often because it doesn't accomplish what the private sector took a pass on. When I was in City Hall, a friend from Wall Street told me, "Business does what's doable, David; government gets all the rest." It certainly presents a no-win situation for government. Government, however, does have more remedies going for it than the private sector. It can use regulations, rationing, patents, copyrights, and prohibitions, and, as we learned again from the 2008 financial swoon, government can exercise some measure of correction and oversight given the sorry performance of market forces and the flawed or corrupt practices of private-sector executives. I recall a privatization episode when I was in City Hall that produced one of those corrupt outcomes that sometimes put the public treasury at risk. The Parking Violation Bureau launched a much touted privatization of its collection effort in order to maximize revenues and to curb public payroll costs. Having emerged from the city's fiscal crisis, the good news of declining unemployment, new public works projects, and the city's return to the private capital markets all served to divert the media's attention from the corruption in the making. Many of the favored private collection firms were not well established or competitive by any market test. They were creatures or allies of Democratic county leaders and their cronies in what was then all but a one-party system in New York City.

Laced throughout the argument for privatization is the insight that *competition* promotes better outcomes than the monopoly machinations of government. And there is something to that when it comes to producing a better product or service. But competition does not necessarily reside only in the private sector. Top-down government can also promote competition if it looks for citizen initiatives that better serve particular communities and might be replicated elsewhere. See what works and where; then see if others find such initiatives a good fit for their social problems as locally viewed. Perhaps we should look to ourselves, flawed as we are, too, rather than choosing sides between the private and public sectors.[31]

Given the popular bias for less government rather than more, are we prepared to step forward to do our part when it comes to social problem solving? It's like the kid in class who talks too much. If he is checked, will we fill the silence? Top-down government trying to solve our social problems is not a good fit.[32] Power *over* is not necessarily power *to* get things done. With all the polling data and expert advice at its command, government comes up short, again and again. We'd like to think someone is in charge and those who ostensibly are will rarely concede they are not.[33] The idea of no one really in charge can frighten us, but it can also liberate us. There never has been nor will there ever likely be one right answer or correct solution for a social problem, much less one public officeholder who can deliver. There are many pathways and many of those pathways lead from all sectors, public, private, and nonprofit, and there is abundant room for each of us, especially if we explore together what we can do. They may be messy, indeterminate courses to follow, but ones that I will show have been far more prevalent throughout American history than many couch potato citizens, or for that matter those who are stakeholders of top-down government, realize.

CHAPTER 2

It's Us . . .

Social Attention and Self-Organizing

When it comes to dealing with social problems of our own making, sure, we can lay them at the feet of top-down government and there will be stakeholders as far as the eye can see trying to find the answers. But since so much depends on our social attention, not theirs, to deal with social problems, doesn't it make sense to start with us, not them? Well, maybe, you say, but a lot of people point the finger at top-down government with its laws and regulations thinking that it has more lasting power to change things. Yes and no. Yes, the powers of government are considerable, but too many of us forget how much we, not government, have done to provide the problem-solving infrastructure in most every community.[1] Where once we had no choice but to do so, now our talents and energy for doing so have stagnated as we repeatedly call upon government to do it for us. In this chapter, I want to recall our self-organizing history so that we not only remember freshly our story but also why and how we can renew that story.

How things happen in our public world, the world we necessarily share with others, is not the story usually told by those in charge or by those in the media who think they know where the action is. We account for the origins of most social problems, their trajectories, and whatever outcomes emerge, whether good or bad. What I think of as our "invisible hand"—the aggregate of our actions or inactions—impacts public health, public safety, public education, race relations, the environment, and so much else. In the web of our private lives, our social attention has established local service clubs, PTAs, historical societies, ambulance corps, volunteer fire departments, veterans' groups, Girl Scouts, 4-H, and the YMCA. From our parochial settings have emerged social movements concerned with abolition, temperance, suffrage, civil rights, and abortions. Think of the shoemakers in Massachusetts who protested work conditions, women in small Midwestern towns who closed down saloons, and Texas farmers who formed cooperative alliances. From local efforts have grown private colleges and universities, voluntary hospitals, libraries, private welfare agencies, churches, and synagogues. Although local associations of kinship, sectarian belief, ethnicity, and occupation are not unique to our country, they have been unusually active and influential here in the absence of enduring forms of social organization based on class, religion, or state control.

When I speak of the web of our private lives, I mean to elevate its importance, which is often diminished by those who think of private life as bound up in narrow self-interest without public consequence. When Rosa Parks refused to move to the back of the bus, how do we distinguish her private life from the public life of Montgomery, Alabama in 1955? We can't. Private life is far more consequential than it is often portrayed and public life is far more accessible. Americans have had essentially two grounds knit together for what they do with their private lives. There is a narrative ground—each person's inheritance of beliefs, and a liberal ground—each person's choices free of any inheritance. These two grounds coexist, often as contending moral claims—the claims we necessarily encounter and the claims we invent. America's public life is largely the private stories of men and women involved and responsible on terms congenial to their everyday lives. For most of us, our private stories will likely be the only public life we have and they will continue to determine the kind of public life we share.

I once watched a young woman enter our village park. She wore dark glasses and nodded to the beat only she could hear on her headset. As she passed the park bench where I was sitting, she tossed aside a can of diet soda, which landed on the grass about 20 feet from a green litter barrel. She walked on nodding to the rhythms of her solitary world. Another young woman pushing a small child in a stroller paused in front of the litter barrel while she finished the ice cream cone that she had been sharing with the child. She took the napkin in which the cone had been wrapped, dropped it into the barrel, and resumed her walk. Finally, I saw a young man, who had been jogging but now walked slowly with hands on hips, spot the soda can, and after glancing my way with just a hint that he suspected it was mine, he deposited it in the litter barrel and continued on. Why does one person litter? Why does another not litter? Why does yet another person pick up other people's litter? If you don't pick up other people's litter, why not? If you do, why, where, and for how long do you do it? Know it or not, each person has what I call a "litter philosophy" arising from his or her social attention or lack thereof. The conditions and problems that each of us encounters in public life are unavoidable, and, like it or not, it means each of us, at one time or another, have to consider the grounds for our participation in public life and the range and likely duration of our participation.

I used to do some litter picking-up on my own in a neighborhood where we once lived. I called it my "litter patrol" and early on Sunday morning I covered about a half mile of state highway. Litter is a very visible social problem, but as more litter piled up, it was impossible to know where it came from and who was responsible for it. I knew if more litter accumulated, people would be even more careless, thinking that one more beer can or fast food bag wouldn't make a difference. As the months passed, hardly anyone seemed to be picking up the mess that others left behind, except me. I knew for sure that I didn't want to spend the rest of my life picking up the litter by myself.

Certainly, litter is a social problem of our own making and, like other everyday problems we encounter, it is beyond anyone's personal effort to rectify. Yes, I can pick up the litter I see, but I know that is far from enough. That is why we look for others to get the job done as many are now doing along their public roads. In a small town where my wife and I lived part of the year, the call went out for volunteers to help with a road cleanup. On an annual basis, families, neighbors, schools, churches, and local companies adopted various sections of non-neighborhood stretches of the main roads. The town provided the trash bags and picked up the filled bags, but most of the heavy lifting was left to folks like us. Volunteers were asked to wear bright-colored clothing and encouraged to take photos of each other so the undertaking could be seen on the town's Web page.

A community is not the source but the sum of actions of those who share mutual problems and live in some proximity to each other.[2] They discover, at one time or another, what natural resources they share, and when social problems arise, like too much litter, they discover what human resources they share. Such human resources don't neatly fit together. It is a hodgepodge of human potential, but at least most of us learn, at one time or another, that our individual resources belong together if we are to deal with social problems effectively. Poet June Jordan once wrote: "We are the ones we've been waiting for," and much of our social history testifies to that—human resources organized and put to the tasks we have identified and acted upon together. So many common practices where we live or work are a consequence of our social attention and self-organizing, sometimes purposeful, occasionally accidental, but of acknowledged and often of enduring value. Think of lost and founds, bulletin boards, auctions, potluck dinners, garage sales, apprenticeships, chaperones, collection plates, car pooling, wildlife refuges, school crossing guards, fairs, parades, time sharing, dating services, designated drivers, living wills, sabbaticals, chain letters, safe houses, hiring halls, insurance pools, consumer credit unions, and on and on.[3] I have compared such outcomes to well-worn paths that we might encounter in an unfamiliar wood we come to. "We don't have to clear a way . . . and well-worn paths, more often than not, get us where we want to go."[4]

Imagine when two hay wagons for the first time arrived at an intersection at the same time. Who went first? The "right of way" not the "left of way" prevailed and thereafter it was in everyone's interest to follow that precedent. Many of our self-organizing practices have long and labored histories, the origins of which we now know very little about, but the evidence is everywhere that once we produce a satisfactory outcome, not necessarily optimal but satisfactory, we adjust and soon take it for granted without a second thought of looking to government or any other central authority for guidance. Consider the neighborhood city sidewalk and "street peace" that Jane Jacobs described in detail where neighbor watches out for neighbor and where strangers may be welcome but whose behavior is monitored. Such everyday social attention from windows and doorways contributes to the public safety of a neighborhood—an example of pure bottom-up self-organizing. Jacobs got it right when she observed that individual actions may seem trivial, but the sum is not trivial at all.[5] It reminds me of what another urban observer, William Whyte, called "a great dance" as he saw pedestrians accommodate each other in the coming and goings on the main floor of Grand Central Station in New York City just as they do on crowded city sidewalks everywhere.[6] Another common incidence of self-organizing is when neighbors come together to oppose a project that they don't want in their neighborhood, which has earned the acronym NIMBY, "not in my backyard." It may involve the siting of a homeless shelter, or a drug rehabilitation center, or a trash-burning incinerator. What is good for others is seen as bad for the neighborhood most affected. In such cases, however, self-organizing is undertaken to resist others' solutions, not to solve the underlying problem.

Self-organizing goes on everywhere you look. Consider the multitude of *acequia* associations in New Mexico that have managed their scarce groundwater resources with the give and take of irrigation ditches shared by adjoining property owners.[7] Or consider the citizens in Kankakee, Illinois who took the abandoned HQ of a private health company and converted it into a public library. The library became the cultural hub of a downtown needing one and was "crucial" in Kankakee's downtown revitalization from which a new bank and satellite university campus emerged.[8] And then there is "slugging," a carpooling undertaking that commuters in the Washington, DC, area put together in which strangers pick up strangers waiting for a ride. Like a train conductor, the driver either calls out his destination or posts a sign in his car window and those in line make their choices.[9] Staying on the subject of car drivers for the moment, too much drunk driving led some mothers to organize and put ribbons on the door handles of the driver's side of the car between Thanksgiving and the New Year in 1986. By 1989, Mothers Against Drunk Driving (MADD) had tied an estimated 40 million ribbons to car handles.[10] Social attention and self-organizing can also spawn new experiments not anticipated as when the women's movement helped to develop Head Start, recreation for the aged, and sheltered workshops for handicapped workers.

We can also learn from the social attention and self-organizing story of City Harvest in New York City, a start-up effort of "ordinary citizens" in the early 1980s who were troubled by seeing so many without enough to eat when so many local restaurants were discarding perfectly good food every day of the week. So they enlisted friends and borrowed cars to transport the leftover food where it was needed most. A simple idea that, with a fleet of trucks, now helps to feed over 260,000 of their fellow New Yorkers each week.[11] When the 2008 recession struck so many lives, City Harvest undertook a special emergency initiative channeling surplus food to a core group of 60 agencies in which demand far exceeded supply. It was not just any food but nutritious food when so many have had to rely on the cheap but unhealthy stuff. City Harvest plays the role of a vital food broker making sure that the abundant surplus of the few is shared with those most in need. I will come back to the City Harvest example in chapter 4.

Social attention and social change rarely come like a thunderbolt from the heavens. They are more organic and their energy and momentum cannot be easily predicted or planned.[12] That is why emerging social practices throughout our history and the potential for new ones are not easily captured here by any blueprint, no matter how thoughtfully laid out. We often do not know their origin and can only guess what other alternatives were considered. We don't know who prescribed them or whether they, more or less, arose spontaneously in response to an incident long forgotten or perhaps never known. No one can say what emerged is the best outcome for a particular problem. There is often competition for how to address a problem and what emerges may be little more than circumstances that made one solution more appealing or convenient than another.[13] Sometimes there are many different outcomes or tentative resolutions rather than one that prevails. After all, it is sometimes very difficult to get agreement on what might constitute a new social practice. Is it congenial to the routines of those needed to make it work? Will some people see it as especially burdensome given their personal work or family circumstances? Does a new social practice make sense in one neighborhood but not another? As I look more closely in chapter 3, all of these questions bear on the crucial question: Will there be enough others to make my effort and your effort worth doing?

Social attention and self-organizing have many different locales. The origin of a new social practice might be traced to the familiar places where people find each other—coffee shops, health clubs, malls, bars, plazas, school auditoriums, church basements, or community college classrooms. In those places, people recount their stories—where they saw the litter or discovered birds strangled by plastic six-pack rings, where perfectly good food is discarded behind a restaurant, where drugs are sold, where latchkey kids hang out, or where the elderly have difficulty crossing the street. From such stories people begin to name problems that are within their range. A community garden might emerge from a give and take about the cost of transported food or the need for better eating habits. The problem of finding adequate plots for such an undertaking and who would tend what would also have to be sorted out. If there is to be a common garden area, what would be grown there? Can the community garden help feed the homeless and just how is that connection made and made to work? How would such a project fit with an existing greenmarket or farmer's market? Or the conversation might turn to putting together a local thrift shop. Some members of a church in town express interest in staffing such an enterprise if some of the profits could go to their church's fund for emergency aid to those who have lost their jobs or are losing their homes through foreclosures. Where could they locate such a shop? What other churches would be willing to staff the thrift shop, and could the thrift shop turn over some of its proceeds to local social service agencies?

The workplace is also a natural intersection for coworkers to sort out their mutual problems and find some way to better coordinate their respective work schedules. With many now living in a dense suburban section close to a large urban center, the problem of commuting has become much worse, especially for working mothers and fathers trying to manage pickups of their children. A "flextime" arrangement won't work unless everyone's schedule can be better accommodated. Is that possible and would it be agreeable to their employer? Water-cooler conversations could also lead to the possibility of day care space at the workplace for preschool children.

Neighbors, friends, and strangers mix at a local gym where the talk can wander from one problem to another. Those working out often need conversation to compensate for the upper body and lower body routines that can be mind-numbing otherwise. Perhaps someone is looking for hospice care for a loved one who is terminally ill. Another has become concerned about a rash of burglaries in his neighborhood and wants to organize a neighborhood crime watch. The conversation on the treadmills goes back and forth between finding hospice care volunteers and finding enough others willing to put some time into the crime watch. There always seems to be talk going on at the gym about forming one support group or another—to cope with loved ones suffering from Alzheimer's, sleep or eating disorders, or the consequences of too much debt.

Wherever and whatever accounts for the emergence of a new social practice, social norms have something to do with sustaining them. Take the case, again, of littering. Without local norms the trash-strewn beaches of Gloucester, Massachusetts once led summer tourists to go elsewhere. Pursuing a counter-intuitive approach, little-used trash barrels were removed and signs that read "No Barrels, No Litter, No Kidding!" were posted. As a consequence, a new social norm was born; local beachgoers cleaned up their act and the beaches stayed clean. The signs, not the litter, got their social attention.[14] Many social practices eventually get codified but the norms that help produce them remain uncodified. Norms are socially constructed without reference to some authority other than enough others make it so. Norms can dictate how to act even though in most cases there may be no consequence if you fail to act properly. Where do these norms and precepts of behavior come from? Their origins are murky but their importance is not. For any new practice to succeed, the expectation is that the social norms of keeping your promises or doing your fair share will prevail.

The Politics of Social Problem Solving

Self-organizing is not driven by feel-good conversations but rather a recognition that very little can get done about a social problem unless we find enough others to deal with it. Consequently, like it or not, we have always been political animals when it comes to addressing social problems. We should not think that politics is something that only politicians do in the precincts of government. Politics is also the give and take between us and among us—anywhere we have differences to sort out and reconcile. Politics describes the way we deliberate in families, with neighbors and coworkers, and wherever differences exist and have to be dealt with. If you were alone on a desert island, there would be no politics. Put just one other survivor there with you and politics becomes necessary. Put a boatload of survivors there on the island with you and politics is not only necessary, it will flourish. The paradox of self-interest ("I want to get off this desert island and why should I care what others want") is that we need the others in figuring out how to get off the desert island.

I think one should be careful around those who say they positively despise politics. They are often those who seek answers and solutions from anyone they think has the power to settle some matter once and for all—leaving no place for the rest of us. Many of us entertain our own grounds for judgment of what should be done about a social problem, but there is rarely any feasible way to enforce anyone's individual preferences in the political life of communities. Whatever our respective technical skills and values, we have to be prepared to adjust them to circumstances over which we have little or no control. Only together can we make decisions or take action. No one should expect that there is one right answer or another. We may not think of ourselves as pragmatists but we are likely to act as if we were. Our behavior is neither self-serving nor public-spirited; it is contingent and, to a great extent, depends on what others do. Our interdependence is an unavoidable circumstance, not a choice. Confronted with a social problem, we may choose to join with others, not because we want to, but because together we have a better chance to produce a satisfactory outcome.

I found in graduate school teaching that politics is rarely practiced in classrooms where authority resides with an instructor who prefers a substantial measure of control. To further keep politics at bay, many instructors establish competitive learning environments where students are tested on their individual abilities to be self-sufficient even though

their real-world experience will teach them something far different—
that little gets accomplished without serious collaboration with others.
I discovered that too much was being done *for* students and not enough
done *by* students. Information and knowledge was packaged and con-
veyed with heavy doses of prescriptive advice derived from abstract
models and quantitative formulae. The problems students were given
came ready-made with enormous amounts of data. Unfortunately, such
excessive packaging obscured the trial-and-error process in which most
learning is grounded.

So my graduate school teaching put students into working groups
so they could experience thinking *with* others, rather than letting me
or anyone else, think *for* them. Given my own experience that taught
me that problem solving is more social than cognitive, I wanted them
to experience what politics is. So I would divide a class into four or
five groups each with the same initial case-story to develop. The story
that evolved had no predetermined outcome. As I received each group's
work, I would build on it and give it back to them for further development. I was trying to simulate real-world conditions in the classroom
that would allow students to actually share in the enterprise of resolving
problems. I didn't want them just to analyze the case as spectators but to
participate in a tentative outcome of their own making, and then to experience the consequences of that outcome by moving on to subsequent
episodes. Such a layered case experience formed a continuous story that
grew more complex but also assumed that students were growing more
politically adept given their increasing familiarity with the social context
in which they found themselves.

I would tell my students:

> It's not enough to think you know what the problem is. It also mat-
> ters what each of those in your group thinks the problem is. It is
> not enough to think you know what the solution is. It also matters
> if the others think that your solution fits their own conceptions of
> what the problem is. And even if your solution does, it is possible
> that they may think that they have better solutions than yours.
> I don't want you to pursue the mistaken belief that an objective
> analysis of a situation is more important than how it appears to the
> others in your group.

They were learning what politics involves, what different outcomes
could develop depending on who they were working with, and how

each group could find its own way to get off its desert island. They were learning not to take for granted that their personal values or preferred problem-solving methodologies could be played as trump cards in their work groups. More important, it was necessary for them to find allies in their group in order to build support for whatever they believed was worth doing. They were learning that they could only get where they wanted to go with the help of others. I would ask them to suspend their own preferences, anticipate the likely preferences of others, concede the differences, and acknowledge that "what works for me has to work for the others too."

I also simulated the "invisible hand," the collective influence of everyday citizens, by staging experiential exercises outside the classroom. For that I created the Factory Hill story, set in an old textile city in New England, where graduate students lived, so to speak, during a semester. In Factory Hill, they confronted the threat of a hostile takeover of the leading employer in town, controversy about the homeless among them, and the civic shock of terrorists taking hostages at the downtown Old Fellows Club. Each semester, two sections, both with approximately 60 students, first analyzed, then entered "through the looking glass" into this public world, and with other role-players produced outcomes in Factory Hill that always varied from one section to another and from one semester to another. The Factory Hill experience dramatized for them that the politics of social problem solving is a complicated and uncertain enterprise with really no one in charge.

Why did I make in-class and out-of-class political exercises so central to my students' learning? I could see that they were fast developing what I called a "professional mind-set" as to how problems should be solved. I wanted to counter this infection which so many contract in their pursuit of professional credentials. Let me explain. I think back to the fall of 2001 when my university in lower Manhattan offered its expertise to those in charge trying to deal with the aftermath of September 11. As far as I could see, there was no special effort being made by the experts in and out of government to connect with residents, small business owners, and displaced workers so they could work together on what should be done. When I mentioned what was missing to a colleague dashing to the elevator, his response was, "Oh, wouldn't that be ideal but you know better than I do, David, that's not the way the system works." He just assumed that with decision makers and their professional advisers already in place that they *were* "the system."

At an earlier stage of my life I was very much a part of "the system" in New York City. Shortly after leaving government, I shared the following with readers of *Change* magazine: "I recall my own pleasure in being called 'a real professional,' presumably someone who is exceptionally competent and self-effacing, when I directed the transition team of the new Koch municipal administration. My counterpart, the deputy mayor of the outgoing administration, offered the compliment at the conclusion of our introductory meeting at City Hall. We were serving very different political leaders and agendas, but first and foremost we were professional colleagues. We knew we were good at what we did and, at that time, that was all that really mattered. For me, being a real professional meant that I was simply not willing to be vulnerable, which may explain why so many dinner parties with professional friends found each of us talking shop endlessly. Without an entrepreneur or an artist at the table, we were capable of putting an entire dinner party to sleep in what Jacques Barzun called 'the dreary exchange of affidavits, which passes for conversation.' "[15]

Fortunately, however, an increasing number of professionals bring a new mind-set to a public world where everyone can contribute. I have learned from the graduate students I worked with and whose careers and lives I have followed that a professional mind-set can be in persistent conflict and capable of dramatic change. There is the partner in a private equity firm in Denver and his wife, an independent documentary filmmaker, who have shared in a "heavy dose of not-for-profit endeavors." A director of policy and planning at a major Hawaiian health insurer shared with me that she was working on her second master's degree, this one in bioethics, via the Internet. From DC came news of a former student now at the World Bank, "restless and undergoing self-examination," and another from Atlanta told me about "seeking balance, creativity, and testing new ground." These are Boomer lives with seemingly endless transitions and they are hungry for fulfillment, which has eluded some of them. They seem more interested in practicality than ideology—believable ways of dealing with social problems about which I have more to say in chapter 4. What they have learned about problem solving is the importance of reaching out to others and treating them as equals in client relationships, sharing as equals their resources with resource-poor communities, and transforming classrooms and organizations from places where "I know better" to "let's learn together." Their example can curb the pretensions of anyone, professional or not, that he knows better without first engaging others and learning together in the ongoing narrative they share. It is a place that too many in government, the large NGOs, and higher education have yet to discover.[16]

Social Movements

Adam Ferguson correctly observed that history is the result of human action, not human design. We often associate design with government laws and regulations, but action usually precedes design. Our history is replete with examples of when citizens, not government, initiated the action. Think of the epic struggles for workers' rights, civil rights, and gender equality. Each such social movement was in response to a status quo seen as no longer tolerable by those most affected, and their self-organizing and bottom-up actions were indispensable in bringing about change.

Economic theory, so wedded to the assumption of self-interest, does not adequately account for history-making social movements. No doubt self-interest broadly understood has been part of any effort to transform others' attitudes on the way to rectifying a particular social problem. When, however, economists deny the efficacy of a strategy that goes beyond self-interest, they tend to ignore several chapters of American history when those aroused made extraordinary sacrifices. Will traditional economic theory now say that something of our own making, new social practices in self-organizing worlds, won't work? Will it assume that such organizing and such practices won't work because they sharply depart from a theoretical assumption? Who cares about the assumption? What one should care about is whether such practices can work. American history offers abundant examples that they can. No guarantees exist, of course, but we have history on our side despite theories that often ignore such evidence. Sometimes something of our own making arises forcefully only when certain conditions and certain events coincide. In the civil rights era, there were those who were waiting for the right bus; their participation was not secured until the right bus came along. They knew where they wanted to go but they couldn't get there until the right vehicle for getting there came into sight.[17]

When we recall historical social movements, the storytelling is certainly not the same as what individuals and groups experienced as they confronted social problems and organized to do something about them. Not that there was a total absence of *intention* at the micro level, only that there was often an absence of intention to coordinate beyond the necessarily limited, transient, local circumstances. Something that *emerges* beyond anyone's control is not part of a master plan that precedes and produces it. That is a major reason why social movements have not had predictable stories. As individuals sought to make a difference regarding a social problem, they knew or quickly discovered that they needed many, many others to make that difference. For example, the labor movement took a long time coming. At first, there were only skilled journeymen and artisans armed with the "labor theory of value" who organized and went on strike, but too few joined them.[18] On the other hand the lunch counter sit-ins of 1960, where four black freshmen at North Carolina A&T were refused service in downtown Greensboro, soon spread to Durham and Winston-Salem. Within a month, students from Florida to Tennessee were challenging segregated lunch counters with the national media taking note. It all depends.[19]

Malcolm Gladwell has argued that the emergence of something significant, a major change—think of a social movement finding its legs—can be analogized to an "epidemic."[20] As individuals see that many others are getting involved, their example becomes contagious. What emerges has no preconceived strategy, no chosen leaders, no predictable storyline. It is many people doing many things but finding each other when their myriad paths cross, and, as a consequence, they coalesce into producing significant social change. With sufficient momentum, people get caught up in the emerging tide of opinion and actions that shape a movement. What once seemed improbable becomes realizable and such a discovery draws many more to take up the cause. The prospect of actual success becomes intoxicating and keeps the momentum going forward.[21] We have only to look at the upheavals in the Middle East in 2011.

With any social practice that gains momentum going forward, no obvious number of adherents will guarantee success. There is no beginning or end to the process and although there are markers of success, each such marker may be more significant to some than to others. I dwell on the concept of emergence, which may seem abstract, in trying to capture why social movements cannot be easily pinned down to time and place, to leaders or followers. They all come in a swirl of events and people. Today, the current Tea Party phenomenon that seeks to shrink the role of the federal government is a movement not easily pinned down.[22] Stories after the fact always develop to explain the path that any significant movement has taken, but such stories and such explanations contain only bits and pieces of a social phenomenon not so easily explained. Storytelling is very important to social movements as those involved recall and retell what happened or what they think happened. Their stories become cumulative and reinforcing, less strange or odd, as they are told again and again with some obvious variations. Like the storytelling of those in power I noted in chapter 1, a social movement is likely to create a narrative with cause and effect and a sequencing of events.[23] Some search for analogies and metaphors like the "wave" that we see or participate in at outdoor stadiums. Obviously, the standing up and sitting down has to start somewhere but very quickly the tide rises, so to speak, as the wave begins to circle the stadium. One person's effort seems trivial but when joined with others, that one person has the delight of seeing quite a sight made possible by others' trivial efforts.[24]

Emergence reminds me of Philip Slater's insight as to why the 1960s produced such enormous and rapid social change. Slater saw individuals converting from "one orientation to its exact opposite" but really only involving "a very small shift in the balance of a . . . persistent conflict."[25] Somewhere along the way the pond turned over. Similarly, 25 years later, Cass Sunstein spoke of "norm bandwagons." Initially, individuals support an existing norm because they fear social disapproval. When such sanctions are no longer so powerful, those who at one time conformed now feel free to support a new norm, perhaps established by a movement they failed to join. Their conversion reinforces the movement's momentum and thus helps to account for a "bandwagon" effect.[26] Another observer has used the term *synergy* to speak of civic energies coalescing around a particular practice. Dan Kemmis thinks "[t]he very concept of synergy is an affront to sharply analytical minds, because synergy cannot be located in any of the parts of what is being analyzed."[27] Although social movements have often involved some personal risk to those who join them, the emergence, the power of a growing social force makes it easier for those who follow. Conformity, not willing cooperation, can be a sufficient motive for those who eventually fall in line and add to the growing numbers of those willing to try something new.[28] I look more closely at the phenomenon of "enough others" in the next chapter.

Many episodes in American history have shown evidence of our potential for bringing about social change from the bottom up. What was so remarkable about the civil rights movement was the overwhelming preference for nonviolence despite the risks and suffering that such a preference had to contend with. Nonviolence was not so much an individual choice as it was a movement choice in dealing with the violence it encountered. It became a strategically moral choice. And the civil rights movement was not just about counting heads and marching downtown. It was about strangers winning the support of strangers by various means not all directly related to the primary cause. For example, members of SNCC (Student Nonviolent Coordinating Committee) went door to door offering to help with chores to overcome the residents' suspicion of young strangers disturbing the affairs of a neighborhood. Social movement stories have usually included such parochial gestures of those who know they need more than just activists like themselves; they also need the social attention of those who stand to one side not sure they want to get involved.

Social movement activists have also sought out those organizations with memberships who can be potential allies. This was the case of the Union League movement during Reconstruction, which drew from a variety of black groups, the women's suffrage movement linked to established women's clubs, and the '60s Free Speech movement at Berkeley with its coalition of student organizations.[29] This was certainly true when a great part of the civil rights movement arose from or became allied with black church congregations—settled groups in communities with many social ties and their own member obligations to get involved, to follow the lead of their pastors, or to take the lead themselves. This is not to say that an organization's members get swallowed up in mass demonstrations and count for very little themselves. Think of Rosa Parks refusing to yield her seat on a Montgomery city bus. Although her dramatic moment was the plan of others, the act of one individual preceded the collective action of many others who followed her example. The Montgomery bus boycott was not so much a sacrifice, but a collective statement of black resolve since most all of those participating were within walking distance to and from their workplaces.[30] As the Montgomery boycott picked up steam, the demands of those involved broadened, which is often true when social movements experience initial successes and the collective energy mobilized leads on to a wider set of demands and actions than originally contemplated.

Some have characterized laborers, blacks, or women as victims relative to those more powerful. But, unfortunately, such a characterization unintentionally diminishes the potential of any disadvantaged group to change the status quo. The problem with putting on the mantle of victim is to assume a dependence on someone else more powerful to solve the problem. Justice may demand it but it can undermine the will to overcome the disadvantage. A further irony is that, as talented individuals at some disadvantage are invited and cajoled to work with those already having power, such individuals can unknowingly undermine a movement that needs their talents more than their well-meaning compromises with those who maintain the advantage. Insiders may bring badly needed help but outsiders may resent insiders trying to fix a social problem when the otherness of outsiders is celebrated and resists being co-opted. While insiders may think such resistance is counterproductive or just plain outrageous, outsiders may recognize their resistance as shrewd and necessary to keep the movement going forward.

Like forest fires that may be spontaneous when there is a lot of dry timber, the fire of a social movement gradually subsides as the dry timber burns out. Movements do not have infinite life—new groups form with rules and laws replacing the spontaneity that a social movement represents. Social movements age and sometimes drift when they succeed in getting top-down government to follow their lead, and the focus on what remains to be done transfers to non-governmental organizations (NGOs). The path followed by social movements is similar to the development of social conventions that arise and take hold but later become law, removing much of the voluntariness required to put them in place. Think of the rules of the road, which predated government taking over the enforcement of those rules through its laws and regulations. It's a natural course—"When the marches, strikes, and late-night meetings fade away, Americans are left with newly legitimated groups, new rules, institutions, and new forms of state authority."[31] Some argue, as William Galston has, that the coercion of the state is necessary, that "vigorous enforcement backed by sanctions has proved essential in changing behavior" from drunk driving to racial discrimination.[32] But the important point that Galston makes does not obviate the important role of social movements that lead the state to become involved in the first place. That is why in chapter 5 I discuss how governments could support emerging social practices, which start with us, not them.

A movement's success can be both a blessing and a curse. Success for a social movement can mean a loss of momentum for those things not yet obtained. No doubt most social problems are too complex to be totally solved and too much clarification through laws and regulations may limit or misshape goals, which can distract or discourage those who thought they had won. Then, too, success has not usually meant reconciliation—blacks with whites, unions with management, women with power holders. In the view of established power holders and those who don't like boat rockers, too much is still asked for and they fail to extend little real acceptance to those who have labored in a movement. Consider the backlash against affirmative action or the taking back of union bargaining rights by fiscally strapped state governments. Still, as movements fade, there are "countless acts of self-assertion" that, for example, women now take for granted "that change the condition and terms" of their daily lives.[33] No small achievement in their post-movement world even though many of them admitted to the main avenues of commerce and professional calling now find it difficult to find the time to organize on their own or others' behalf.

There is, however, a never-ending social movement involving the millions of those giving their social attention to the degradation of the natural environment. The concept of sustainability has become the measure and goal of those working both alone and together. I will not dwell on this massive, decentralized, and ongoing undertaking because others are already writing so much and doing so much—my focus is on other social problems. It seems unlikely that the sustainability movement will age and wither—the goals are so ambitious, so far from realization that the work goes on with or without government support. It remains decentralized, not by choice but by necessity, given its varied agenda bound up with time and place across the globe.[34]

Clay Shirky in his important book, *Here Comes Everybody,* explains why he thinks both old and new social movements are always possible in these times: "We are living in the middle of a remarkable increase in our ability to share, to cooperate with one another, and to take collective action, all outside the framework of traditional institutions and organizations."[35] Changing a culture and the attitudes that sustain it is never easy. It can be a very complicated process and, in fact, a culture may be only comprehended fully when there are those who try to change it. We should not for a minute think that any story can end with a "they lived happily ever after" coda. As much as we would wish otherwise, social attention and self-organizing are never ending.

CHAPTER 3

. . . And Enough Others

Enough Others

Given our political heritage, my argument is that the social attention and self-organizing of enough citizens and the momentum of their example can still generate substantial social change. Some object that local efforts don't dent a nationwide social problem and, understandably, the problem overwhelms them on such terms. Such thinking, however, distracts too many given the decentralized era we have entered with the flattening of organizational hierarchies and the open architecture of the Internet. As one keen observer foresaw, it should be a seismic shift in "the way we see and construct the world."[1] Information is spread far and wide—instantaneously. It is subject to analysis and interpretation by millions. Even though such information dissemination is radically new, decentralization, as a given in our ever-changing social and political order, is not really new. We have a rich history of contentious federalism and the separation of powers on the government side of the street and the tides of immigration, local initiatives, and national mobilizations on the citizen side. Using Chris Anderson's analogy, think of our current era of decentralization as a dropping water line revealing what has always been there yet newly emerging.[2] Nonetheless, the old American habit of social attention and self-organizing, as recounted in chapter 2, now confronts new circumstances in a decentralized era that is not like any time we have experienced before. We remain entangled but less attached.[3] If we are to be the real change-makers again, can we find enough others to make a real difference?

Enough others is a simple way to describe what is not a simple proposition; it is a threshold, but without any predetermined number that anyone can know in advance. Like producing a standing ovation in an opera house, it all depends. There are many examples of the enough others dynamic in our everyday comings and goings. Consider trying to cross a busy thoroughfare. If enough of us band together to halt car traffic turning right in the intersection, we can reach the other side of the street—safely. Or consider how we then stand in line at a ticket booth. Our line does not so much solve the problem of congestion as provide a way to deal with it, if enough others go along with the idea. We self-organize by forming the line and we enforce the convention ourselves when someone comes along and tries to crash our line. We rightly consider his conduct is "out of line" with those of us who go along to get along. After all, the longer we stand in line the more time we have invested in making it work and getting to the front. And then there is the street entertainer who we come upon down the block. What he needs is a few people stopping by to watch and listen in order to get others to stop by, too. As early birds, we're drawn to his performance and linger to watch and listen. Then other passers-by see us and come over to see what's going on. As others passing see the crowd growing around the entertainer, more of them take the time to join us. The entertainer smiles. Now he has enough others, and his hat soon fills with coins and dollar bills. It's the same when we decide to go look for a good restaurant. The empty place around the corner with its table settings at the ready but no one eating there turns us off. When we walk on and find a crowded eatery, the many already there draw us in. "This must be a good place," we say, "or why would all these people be here in the first place?" "Let's try it!" And so we join them, just as others did when they saw us drawing close to the street entertainer.[4]

Relating enough others more directly to visible social problems, imagine someone lying near the curb of a busy city street with pedestrians hurriedly passing by. Then someone pauses and stops to investigate, and suddenly others take notice and stop to help too. One person goes for water, another for food, and someone else looks for assistance from a passing patrolman. Similar to the street entertainer, the stricken soul at the curb merited little attention until enough others took notice.[5] Our public behavior should not be characterized as self-serving or public-spirited . . . it all depends, and it often depends on if enough others are already involved to get us to join them. I think back to a terrible December snowstorm in Denver where we were living at the time. There were not enough municipal snow plows to get the side streets cleared and most residents stayed hunkered down inside waiting for the plows that never came. So they complained bitterly about being kept from their holiday shopping and necessary errands. Without enough others in a neighborhood going outside to clear the walks, driveways, and streets themselves, the residents saw no way to get to the supermarkets and Wal-Marts. Every person counted, but if they couldn't see enough others out there already shoveling, most stayed put inside. While no less unhappy, some hearty souls did step outside, and, here and there, organized their block to shovel and plow themselves out of driveways, down side streets, and on to the main arteries. For them, the public world was not centered in City Hall but what they did with others to get their wheels rolling again. To be sure, *what* was missing were enough municipal plows but, equally true, *who* was missing in most neighborhoods were enough residents taking it upon themselves to help get the job done, one way or another. It is much the same when neighborhood lights dim and then a blackout occurs. The lights may not go on again until enough others call to rouse the utility company that something major needs fixing. Enough of us calling, enough of us shoveling—it's a simple proposition. It is not that we become selfless; it is that we become empowered together to solve problems far beyond any individual's capacity to solve on his own.

Beyond a core group who gets things started, the eventual success of self-organizing does not rely on knowing all of those who join in. The success is in the numbers, enough others who can make a substantial difference, which means self-organizing centered on regularities of behavior, not just relationships. The gathering momentum of a new social practice can be compared to a forest fire. How much the fire travels and how much it consumes depends far less on its origin than on the circumstances and dynamic of how it develops. "The nature of the fire does not depend on the original source of the heat."[6] Still, it's worth considering how any new social practice catches fire. One spark, as a source of heat, was identified by Alexis de Tocqueville long ago when a citizen might conceive of some need not being met and then go across the street to discuss it with his neighbor. "[T]hey seek each other out, and when found, they unite. Thenceforth they are no longer isolated individuals, but a power conspicuous."[7] Going across the street to talk to a neighbor is still a place to start, but in this day and age the outreach can be much greater, has to be much greater, to make a social difference. Where do we find enough others to make bottom-up change more than just a topic of blog talk? After all, some things worth doing are just not worth doing unless we can find enough others to join in.

NGOs

One modern avenue for finding enough others is the major role of local, regional, national and international non-government organizations (NGOs), whose agendas often mirror our own interests in getting something done about one social problem or another. The growth of many NGOs in our time partly resulted from many activists turning away from government and preferring NGOs which have the professional self-confidence that they can get the job done with enough staff and special-interest advocates working the hallways and aisles of top-down government. This "third sector," according to one source, accounts for 10 percent of U.S. employment with 1.5 million of them having combined assets of $500 billion.[8] Many heavyweight NGOs use "federated structures" to mobilize support through local branches with member dues and contributions helping to finance their agendas and member names on the petitions they carry to city halls, state houses, and inside the Beltway.[9] The petition campaigns are not just to impress stakeholders inside the Beltway that an NGO has the numbers behind it; they also serve as a device to reinforce their members' commitment to the cause.

So what is the downside to delegating social attention to NGOs that ostensibly stand in for their members? Well, first, contributions and petitions don't get many off the couch to become active themselves. Furthermore, NGOs are established organizations manned by professionals who think in most instances that they know better than their members how social problems can be solved.[10] For example, when I went back to look at what John Javna had done to update his 1989 *50 Simple Things You Can Do to Save the Earth*, I found his 2008 edition to be the cumulative result of what NGOs had told him to include. He was no longer the source himself for his readers.[11] Sometimes, there is little difference between the NGO professional mentality and the mentality of those in top-down government who think of themselves as professionally equipped to problem solve with others of like background. The calculation of goal-setting supported by analysis and planning is taken for granted within a large NGO and the expectations of major supporters. Among social commentators, Theda Skocpol has probably come closest to painting an accurate picture of how NGOs have left us out of social problem solving. She takes note that most grant-making foundations and think tanks do not even have members, but rely on their "money or expertise to influence public life." Those elite circles are "much more focused on specialized, instrumental activities than on broad expressions of community or fellow citizenship." Reinforcing the professional distance of NGOs from their lay publics are grant makers who "prefer professionally run groups for their expertise and stability."[12] And, no doubt, grant maker money talks. A consensus reigns that professionals have the requisite knowledge of how government works—the maze and complexity of regulations and funding—that is beyond citizen interest or capacity. Implicit is the assumption that we can find answers to our social problems in such a professional world. Skocpol calls it "doing for others" rather "doing with others."[13]

NGOs often represent the middle age of social movements. The evolution of what was once raw and vigorous self-organizing leads on to a well-intended organization where the social problem has been addressed, but far from solved. Unfortunately, preserving the organization can sometimes become more important than the original impulse for change. Like for-profit organizations, or government agencies for that matter, NGOs become the property of those who organize and run them. A 2009 study of NGOs, "The Organization-First Approach," found that "engagement . . . is usually defined in terms of the needs and interests of their organizations and not those of the community." One NGO leader was quoted as saying, "I'm not evaluated by how well I involve people. Keeping my job depends on what we get done." Another said that NGO organizations "were evaluated strictly by outcomes." One NGO leader said: "We know what works. The challenge is convincing the community what works." Such an attitude is, in part, conditioned by what another leader called an "elusive public." The study concluded that all of this "prompts organizations [NGOs] to adopt solutions and practices that they feel will gain internal support they can control, and they are confident in implementing."[14]

So NGOs are not necessarily a safe bet to lean on. Besides, when the resources of some NGOs are limited, that limitation can misshape their agenda as they seek support from those with deeper pockets than those of most individual members, or NGOs become so result-oriented that they lack the patience to develop the capacities of the particular clientele they serve. Given the relatively closed professional circles of the NGO world, where are more hospitable places that can enlarge our social attention, extend self-organizing, and make it possible for us to find enough others? There are some obvious places I call "social scaffoldings."

Social Scaffoldings

When I was president of a small college, the lack of faculty interaction across departments troubled me. Faculty members had lost touch with one another even in that small place. How could I find a way to create new intersections where they would meet without their feeling that some administrator was being manipulative? So I decided to put a coffee pot and the departmental mail in a spot where faculty would run into each other on a daily basis. My hope was that the new coffee/mail intersection would create a spontaneous occasion for conversations; where projects across departments might hatch; where better acquaintance might lead to new academic practices that might be shared. And new projects did emerge from the coffee/mail intersection, which was only scaffolding, but essential in prompting faculty collaborations that were of their making, not mine. A social scaffolding is not design nor does it offer control but, instead, offers a place for most everyone and the potential of yielding better outcomes than perhaps anyone in charge can conceive.[15]

Some of our more prominent social scaffoldings include social media and various networks, which digital technology now connects so effortlessly; local club and church memberships, which develop loyalties and prompt members to each do their part; and public spaces, which help bring strangers together. Social scaffoldings are for standing on to build something, but they are hospitable to a wide range of uses. It would be a mistake to assume that those who come together in a network, or as members, or in a public space come there for the same reasons or with the same expectations. Scaffoldings provide useful supports for social attention and self-organizing but there is no guarantee that will happen. Can the fitful attention of those online really sustain bottom-up change? What about the decline in face-to-face membership when so many multitaskers live and work with few ties to others and their time is a precious commodity? And it's apparent that there is an underutilization of public spaces for exchange and deliberation when so many commercial interests compete for our attention by promoting an entertainment and sports culture to consume what free time we have. Social scaffoldings offer considerable opportunities but currently face formidable obstacles.

Networks

There are all kinds of networks. Those that get the headlines are not ones we would care to emulate—terrorist groups, drug cartels, and street gangs. The social network that appeals to most of us these days, and, for some, consumes most all of their free time and attention, is the Internet. Who can deny the current hyper-interest in the vast potential of the networks that the Internet enables and sustains? About 20 years ago, the Internet linked approximately 20 million users, 1 million computers, and 70,000 registered networks. Now more than 1.5 billion people use its services across the globe with few physical boundaries that constrain the reach of social attention and self-organizing. Even though much has been written about the wonders and potential of this online world, we sometimes forget that as human beings we have not changed that much even though the online world is an unending environment of change. I am no different in wanting to explore its possibilities here while remaining skeptical that we will grasp and use many of them. Granted, if people need to know how others are choosing before making their own choices, it matters whether they can find out what everybody else is doing.[16] Such reach and volume in the digital world, however, is like drinking from a fire hose. Only so much can be absorbed, an awful lot is wasted—the day's torrent of information lying in vast puddles.

Building networks online is very different from building those that occupy some particular physical space. It can sometimes be difficult to *trust* both the information and its sources online, and it may take considerable time to distinguish the bogus from the workable. In this peer-dominated electronic world, *reputation*, yours and mine and that of a multitude of strangers we encounter online, becomes very important if we are to develop a trust about each other's motives and entreaties. Although each of us has some measure of control over what reputation we project to others, reputation is also democratically constructed, so to speak, by the opinions of others with whom we have only limited influence. Trust is not easily established among strangers when there are no other ties. No doubt, a social problem itself and mutual interest in doing something about it can develop ties, and as a young generation finds it easy to operate online, perhaps trust will become less important, at least in social niche sites where group identity is more or less taken for granted and serves as a substitute for personal trust. We know that it can dramatically tie people together in a crisis whether in Cairo or Tehran, although as one young Iranian living abroad noted, "[F]ighting a government as determined as the Islamic Republic of Iran will require much more than the Facebook fan pages, Twitter clouds, and emotional YouTube clips."[17] Those in Cairo might disagree. Trust, however, for many online users still counts a lot as they struggle to maneuver in a digital world that includes hackers, identity thieves, and other such ilk. Even eBay's founder learned that without community norms that lie outside the phenomena of eBay itself, the enterprise was threatened by those who would exploit it rather than adapt to what the great majority of users wanted or expected in their exchange of goods.

When describing networks some observers graphically draw lines from one node to another in what is a maze of lines and nodes. That is why some blogs and Facebook pages have found such an important place as nodes of opinion that are shared, whatever the subject. Such nodes, however, are less action-oriented as opinion-driven. John Seely Brown and Paul Duguid observed that "much of the 'infosphere' continues to resemble one of those open-mike poetry readings in New York bars where everyone comes to read and very few to listen."[18] Where everyone comes to voice their opinions whether or not anyone else is paying attention makes the Internet medium less consequential than what many would like it to be. With some important exceptions, like the firestorms in the Middle East that digital technology helped to enable, self-interests online are served, but what is usually lacking in such a thin form of communication is a collective resolve to work together on social problems. Few may be listening, and, for those who are, it is so easy to exit in their hurry to travel far and travel fast online. Again, like the poetry reading analogy, more come to speak than to listen, and certainly not to self-organize.[19] In fact, blogs often react to what others produce rather than producing anything of their own making. They rely on news sources and churn out opinion much like customer reviews on Amazon and elsewhere. Their method is not that different from traditional broadcasting—essentially one-way communication with a range of niche audiences. Jason Lanier describes this phenomenon as "a culture of reaction without action."[20] Still, with those on Facebook and other social outlets learning from each other, who knows what they might or can do when they get up and get out in the actual world? There is still only sporadic evidence, however, that they are ready to walk their talk.

Nonetheless, considerable potential remains for social attention and self-organizing online. For example, Googling provides an extraordinary intersection where we can find information using the criterion that what others prefer helps us sort out what each of us prefers.[21] There is also the practice of crowd sourcing, which has social applications offering some collective potential that individual surfing ignores or neglects. Crowd sourcing is tasked to an undefined public whereas open source, which has gone beyond its non-proprietary software origins, usually includes only a qualified group of participants. What is commonly assumed by those who write about the Internet and practice what they preach is the bottom-up nature of the medium. For commercial uses, Chris Anderson is almost euphoric: "The new tastemakers are us. Word of mouth is now a public conversation, carried in blog comments and customer reviews, exhaustively collated and measured. The ants have megaphones."[22] The problem remains, however, is anybody listening, or, more to the point, are enough others not only listening, but getting organized? Michael Sandel would redirect the attention to ourselves, not the Internet. "Converting networks of communication and interdependence into a public life worth affirming is a moral and political matter, not a technological one."[23]

Memberships

> To be attached to the subdivision, to love the little platoon we belong to in society, is the first principle (the germ as it were) of public affections.
>
> Edmund Burke

We have traveled far from Burke in our expansive continent and modern time, but parochial settings and experience are still important intermediaries. There are more than 500,000 local churches and synagogues across the country, all manner of local clubs, associations, and action groups, and still growing numbers of homeowner associations, albeit with covenants, conditions, and restrictions.[24] There is a substantial difference between traditional membership associations and modern NGOs. NGOs usually exercise a great deal of control in what is done and how it is done, while voluntary associations operate largely through consent.[25] What we learn from such associations is to be part of something larger than ourselves. Being a member helps to clarify what is expected of us, but it does not necessarily mean that our membership ties are deeply personal or long-lasting. Nonetheless, our country has always been more a dynamic enterprise of diverse private associations making their demands on us than a nation-state capable of defining our public duties.

That small college in my home state of Illinois offered me the opportunity, as its president, to renew the college's long-established work program, a membership experience of the first order, where each student contributed 15 hours a week to help operate the campus. Soon after arriving, I joined a student work group assigned to various maintenance jobs. An excerpt from a reporter's visit to my office describes one day in that story:

After coming off his work detail on Wednesday, he hurriedly suited up for a meeting with corporate executives who were bearing gifts for the college.

"VIPs don't like to wait for presidents who are picking up trash," he explained. . . .

. . . Later Wednesday Brown underwent another change of clothing, donning full academic regalia—a scarlet gown and clanking metal necklace (which he says put him in mind of the Ghost of Christmas Past)—for his first presidential address to the campus. . . . [H]e found a special significance, not to mention downright glee, inadvertently being part of the work crew that helped prepare the auditorium for his speech.

"I actually carried in my own chair that I'll sit in for the convocation," he said.[26]

Why did I care? The prevailing learning environment in higher education tests students on their competitive abilities to survive alone. The work program experience offered a different kind of education. I knew that to be really empowered requires that students empower each other through the membership and the daily enterprise they share. It was a membership experience in which each student contributed his or her time to the college as together they discovered how much they needed each other to get the campus work done. My thinking at the time was that students needed such a discovery, perhaps for the first time, of what it means to be a member of a community. Of course, service learning is one option many colleges and universities provide for individualized off-campus experience in the surrounding community. But I saw no reason why a college should not have its own work and service agenda shaped and debated by all its members in which students were expected to participate on behalf of the college—the essence of what membership is. I continue to believe that striving for an exemplary community through active membership, however imperfect and confused, is an educational experiment that should be tried and tried again. Very few colleges and universities get it right, and there are, at any one time, only a handful even trying. There should be more. Too many students treat campus life as if they were in a shopping mall with nothing expected of them except to pay the bill. College life may be the first and last time when there can be an intentional effort to have students be part of a community and learn what it means to be a member, to look out for more than just themselves.

These days, surfing the Web and pursuing commercial entertainment can leave little time for shared membership experiences. As time permits is becoming the new standard for the entertainment-absorbed, multi-tasking set. Finding enough time for social attention and self-organizing, not to mention finding enough others, is especially difficult for working women, and some men, trying to handle parenting and all that goes with it. Many do not stay put in any community for very long. School vouchers permit them to choose a school for their kids and employment opportunities may beckon them to relocate again and again. Many factors make their time and attachment to the demands of one place at one time very tenuous. They scatter themselves in a variety of pursuits, acting as self-starters rather than as responsive members of any organization. What social contacts they make, besides at the workplace, is what Robert Wuthnow characterizes as "loose connections" providing valuable, if unpredictable ways, to get involved in specific projects before moving on. Such projects capture their attention and resonate with their own personal values but have little to do with the tacit obligations arising from memberships. One of those with only loose connections told Wuthnow that "the people I know are my community."[27]

So living in a time when many choose their respective communities, there is an argument to be made for "loose connections" or "weak ties."[28] Although such self-segregated communities may not be conducive to bringing unlikes together, there will always be those who search through their networks to find new connections and new ties, instead of relying on the same old circle of friends. Weak ties can connect them with wider circles of acquaintance, which, if mobilized, can break them out of homogeneous patterns, which traditional memberships often reinforce as well.[29] Certainly, in our large cities, weak ties can be more than sufficient as citizens learn from their urban experience the necessity for collective action given the close quarters and dense neighborhoods they live in. Jane Jacobs, the quintessential observer of city life, saw that, like it or not, city dwellers learn that neighborhoods work better when strangers look out for each other even though their ties lack "kinship or close friendship or formal responsibility."[30] When so many social problems are so visible every day, urban spaces with weak ties can sometimes promote working relationships for the public good and still permit residents to move on and disengage themselves from others when they think their work is done. I should add that weak ties can become far more than just a means of finding enough others to get the job done. In many temporary undertakings, finding each other can be an end in itself. That was what I found in many political and civic campaigns, which were certainly goal-driven but also created temporary social bonds unrelated to the campaign's goal. In the case of a political campaign, the loser's HQ and the winner's HQ on election night were not that different as partisan colleagues regretted that their time together was coming to an end. Victory or defeat had very little to do with how they felt about each other.

Unfortunately, small, tight-knit neighborhoods and communities where memberships endure and weak ties are less common may lack the self-sufficiency more evident in such social clusters in the past. Such places have become entangled with county, state, and federal agencies for reasons of funding and government regulations. As compensation, individual citizens have gained greater access to government, bypassing their need for mobilizing local memberships to get the attention of bureaucrats and politicians. Certainly when individual rights are involved, a lawyer or lobbyist may prove handier in gaining attention and resolution of a grievance. Recourse and reliance on freedom of information policies, sunshine laws, public hearings, public notice, and comment requirements are just some of the access sources to which individual citizens can turn.[31] If membership, then, is no longer the leverage needed in many places, social attention and self-organizing across websites and across workplaces becomes even more important as citizens find them more compatible with their self-interests as they become part of various social ecologies without strong community ties.[32]

Public Spaces

Public spaces, such as bars and parks, barbershops and drugstores, porch steps and street corners, have always been where people find each other, where stories and opinions are shared, where they talk about social problems, talk through them, and sometimes get beyond the talk to a resolve to do something about them—to walk their talk. Harry Boyte has long seen public spaces as important places where "people are able to learn . . . a deeper and more assertive group identity, public skills, and the values of cooperation."[33] Public spaces are not necessarily where groups form and agendas develop. Those who frequent such places may have no particular social ends in mind at all, but whatever public spaces exist they remain intersections where we can learn about social problems, where we can share opinions about them, and maybe, just maybe, something can develop. Some of us make good use of whatever parochial spaces are available. Some of us don't. Claude Fischer uses the term "parochial space" as something "chosen not imposed." Fischer traces the ebb and flow of public spaces starting with early American settlements as essentially "encouraging" private life; then in the 19th century more public spaces emerged with city streets, department stores, and amusement parks, followed by a retreat in the 20th century to private homes and more selective social groups.[34]

As more and more couch potato citizens shut their front doors to the public world and stay inside to entertain themselves with various media, public spaces have lost considerable influence in helping us find enough others. The idea of public spaces has also been compromised of late by the desire to limit the daily intersections we might share with others in our neighborhoods. Gated communities and the restrictive covenants of homeowner associations dictate who can do what and where. There seems to be less interest in providing and sharing public spaces. Many housing developments have plenty of driveways but no sidewalks at all. People jump in their cars and off they go. They may wave to a neighbor from their car window but in an instant they are around the corner and gone. Too many public spaces are neglected as people proceed on in their cars to get to work, or to get somewhere other than linger where they might learn from others as others might learn from them. Yes, they have destinations like Starbucks and shopping malls, but too many use them for private pursuits rather than as public spaces where social problem solving can get started. Anywhere there are cafés, communal tables, bookstores, and such, there are always public spaces for those who seek company and the opportunity to share whatever is on their minds. That is, if they can put aside the laptop for a moment. I'm always struck by how little conversation seems to be generated in those places wired for computers; most everyone sips their brew and lingers over their laptop in silence.

Older villages and cities, however, do not mimic the suburban or ex-urban car culture. Nearby where we now live in northern New Mexico, there is a village community center, a public space, which plays host to a range of activities—a gallery or studio tour, a historical talk by a local historian, volunteers needed to catalog and barcode library acquisitions, memorial luncheons after the death of a loved one, an arts and crafts fair, an alcohol recovery program, ceramic classes, two quilting groups, and so on. Regardless of what activity is hosted, people find each other there. In New York City, where I lived and worked for many years, an abundance of public parks, mass transit, storefronts, and, of course, city sidewalks, remain vital places where things happen, both good and bad, in the chaotic but attractive public spaces they offer.

Greenmarkets have gained a following, too, and serve various purposes for people finding each other, as well as fresh produce. I think of New York City's Union Square that draws considerable numbers to its greenmarket but also served as an important public space immediately after September 11. What I saw both day and night that September in the Square and its park were strangers expressing an urgent need to communicate their feelings and thoughts in a public space with public witnesses. It was apparent and understood among those who sat cross-legged in small groups or stood in circles that it was not enough, or even bearable, to grieve alone. Men and women of all ages came to Union Square to share their fear as well as their sorrow—lighting candles, holding hands, and writing messages of hope, despair, and anger on makeshift canvas and poster board. They read each other's posted messages, sang, prayed, and, in unaffected communion, tried to make sense of what had happened and what should be done. The public space they shared made it possible. I'll come back to that moving story in chapter 5.[35]

Obstacles to Finding Enough Others

Whatever the venue, social scaffolding or not, there are obviously many obstacles in getting enough others' social attention and willingness to do their part about the social problems at hand. Couch potato citizens offer a number of excuses: "I don't know enough," or "I can't make a difference," or "I've got better things to do."

"I don't know enough" comes easily in our culture of professionalism. Some argue that our social problems are too complicated for the average Jack and Jill to sort out and that it's better to delegate such problems to the experts, whether in top-down government or NGOs, who know more, know better . . . well, you know the argument. But such delegation, ongoing since the Progressive era a century ago, hasn't worked out as expected. That's why so many are now up in arms about the cost of government, the regulatory red tape, and the persistent arrogance of those who like their expert status but who are way over their heads when it comes to solving social problems without us. The professional mind-set often ignores the historical evidence that solving social problems requires the collective potential of many hearts and minds. For all of us, "I don't know enough" is often quite true, but it becomes a careless evasion when we think that there are others who do know enough, thereby letting us off the hook. As for those who think otherwise, like

Dorothy, they are likely to discover just a little man behind the screen in the Throne Room of the Great Oz.[36]

"I can't make a difference" is an excuse with considerable irony given how each of us has been educated to succeed on his own only to find that self-reliance is clearly inadequate when it comes to doing something about social problems. Unbridled individualism certainly does not mis-shape human nature, but offers very little help for social problem solving. The reflex of going it alone only offers "bewilderment and political impotence."[37] Too many hark back to a time in our early history when those on new frontiers had little choice but to fend for themselves. To praise such self-reliance then is understandable, but to praise it now, as sufficient in an increasingly interdependent world, is romantic nonsense. Even back then in the good old days, self-reliance often sought out help from others in barn raisings, fraternal organizations, and immigrant-aid societies.[38] Even those we think of as self-made are few and far between. Most of us, whatever our rise and accomplishments, have benefitted from parents, friends, and mentors. Our accomplishments have not just been of our own making. "We cling to the idea that success is a simple function of individual merit."[39] An erroneous idea indeed.

The community model that I advanced in my teaching and referred to in the preceding chapter went against the grain of radical individualism rooted in our history and culture. I made the effort, however, because the self-reliant model in higher education just does not address the powerlessness that so many graduates encounter despite their hard-won and costly professional credentials, which they thought would be empowering. "Empowering" is sort of a useless term unless we are ready to empower each other through shared forms of membership or networked enterprise. The self-reliant, credentialed model so many students now pursue and embrace is driven, in part, by the admirable desire to be useful in an ever-changing public world, but such a model represents a failure of social imagination to explore what that world might become when those with or without credentials work together as equals. Such work would have much in common with those who join self-help groups. The very name "self-help" embraces a contradiction: "I want to do something myself, but I need others' help."

To those who say "I've got better things to do," my response would be "Like what? Sitting around entertaining yourself silly?" No doubt all of us free ride at one time or another when we stand to benefit from what others do instead of joining with them. Again, in my teaching I would focus on why and when free riding can be an issue, and I used an exercise in class to demonstrate. I handed each of my students an envelope in which they could choose to put any amount of money or none at all before they returned the envelopes to me. I told them if the amount of money returned to me totaled more than $20, each would get $2 (assume, for the moment, that there were 20 students in the class), but I also told them that there could be no communication among them while each decided what to do. If they thought about it, the free rider choice seemed to dictate not putting any money in the envelope. They risked losing no money while preserving the opportunity of getting some for themselves if their fellow students put enough money in their envelopes to meet the $20 target. But the more they thought about it, if everyone used the same reasoning, the target amount would not be met and no one would get anything—there would be nothing to free ride on. It became even more complicated, however, because if you contributed your fair share, in this case $1, but others did not, the target amount would probably not be met and you would be the loser. If you contributed more than your fair share, let's say $2, it still might not be enough and, anyway, you would not stand to gain anything. Certainly the students understood the weakness of any undertaking if there was not an adequate opportunity to communicate with those trying to decide what to do. For the record, too many chose to free ride and I never had to part with my money in the many times I conducted the exercise.

Some of those with better things to do look to top-down government for direction or think it's simply a matter of kicking the bad guys out of office and replacing them with good guys, even though social change is more complicated than just voting for one team or another and then, as spectators, cheering on one side or another. To make matters worse, other couch potato citizens think government exists primarily to advance their self-interests, either as victims seeking legal relief or as beneficiaries in need of top-down government's deep pocket. They rarely question their centralized mind-set because it's easier to find one cause for their troubles or one source for their support. For many, bottom-up organizing is just too costly in personal time or effort, and with dollar contributions replacing time, they support NGOs or do nothing at all.[40]

For those with better things to do, some prefer to exit the scene, hoping to find a place where a particular social problem is less evident. "In a real sense physical flight is the American substitute for the European experience of social revolution."[41] Fight or flight for many is a relatively easy choice—better to move on than stay and have to deal with the problem at hand. In deteriorating neighborhoods, those with talent and options often go first. Or with schools in decline, the search is for better ones somewhere else.[42] The irony is that as the federal government has superseded local and state governments as the primary source for throwing money and regulations at social problems, citizen exits become less tenable as taxes and enforcement reach them wherever they go.

Overcoming the Obstacles

Yes, too many couch potato citizens with too many excuses present innumerable obstacles in finding enough others, but such obstacles are not insurmountable. Social attention and self-organizing can still lift off and go in many directions with a variety of approaches to solving a problem as a variety of core groups pursue what they think will work—competing sometimes but learning from each other in parallel rather than sequential development—a mélange of activists and bystanders, ideologues and pragmatists, young and old. Such change-makers needn't be, shouldn't be, choosy, looking only for those they like or who are like them. Social change is not a niche art form. Rather it is a messy, indeterminate story without end.

So the overcoming often starts with a core group—those who get things started and stay with it. They are what we might call "unconditional cooperators." They have reasons to act or attachments to others that do not require the same incentives those coming later may need. They are unequivocal in their commitment and their influence is likely to be disproportionate to their numbers. They may very well have experienced successful self-organizing in the past for a cause that engaged them.[43] The members of a core group may have worked together before in a cleanup, crime watch, food pantry, carpool, recycling center, day care site, or elderly outing in the community. They may want to sustain relationships, preserve reputations, or reciprocate past favors. They may also be located in various neighborhoods, workplaces, churches, and local associations or form their ties online. In any event, they are a core group seeking to recruit others. To use earlier analogies of mine again, they are there with the street entertainer, regardless of crowd size; they enter the restaurant because they know what they want whether or not others are already eating there; they simply believe that someone has to be the first off the curb into traffic to mobilize others to follow and create the safety in numbers needed to get across to the other side, and they know that to get where they are going they need the help of enough others.

After the unconditional cooperators come the "conditional cooperators." Conditional cooperators are not there at the outset but are likely to piggyback on an enterprise already under way. Unconditional cooperators may try to find less demanding tasks for those who are more hesitant. You don't put someone in the deep end of the pool if they are not prepared to take the plunge unequivocally like those in the core group. Conditional cooperators need more time in the shallow end to get accustomed to the water. Perhaps they can do their own thing in the shallow end without having to compare their dog paddling with the deep-diving porpoises in the deep end. Strangely enough, their conditional cooperation can be a strength, not a weakness. Think of it this way: if everyone else is committed, why do they need you? If, however, your cooperation is important for enlisting or maintaining the cooperation of others, then you become important, not merely an accessory. Most of us are conditional cooperators. We may think of ourselves as team players, good neighbors, or just good sports. We usually try to go along to get along, but how far and how long we join in is often an open question. That's why enough others taking part can be extremely important to us as conditional cooperators. We don't want to feel that we are on a fool's errand. We would like to see progress. Why not? Who wouldn't? Some take part only after they can see that enough others have already done so. They bring up the rear, so to speak. Others take part until they see that too many don't. Then they drift away. And, of course, many remain somewhere in the middle between the cautious and the brave.

A core group comes to realize the difference between what they want and what those in the middle may think is possible. For a core group, taking a stand for what they want is not enough. Members of the core group should also stand in the other person's shoes, the shoes of those in the middle. I used to tell my students that there is a big difference between allies and finding enough others. Allies work with you; enough others is the number you need in order to succeed. I would say, "See your liftoff in two stages: the booster phase is getting off the launching pad with your allies; enough others gets you into orbit."[44] To find enough others, the core group needs to remember that what works for them to some degree has to work for those in the middle too.

What incentives or stratagems are available to keep the many in the middle engaged? The repertoire includes

(1) *experiencing a particular social problem,* not just thinking about it;
(2) *striving to solve the problem,* which for some can become an end in itself;

(3) *deputizing specific tasks* for those who may otherwise drift away; and

(4) *offering lots of feedback* by talking up *small wins* and exaggerating the *prospects of success* to those who remain tentative about an undertaking.

(1) *Experiencing a social problem*: By now you know my mantra is that problem solving is more social than cognitive. Just thinking and talking about a problem is usually too limiting and yields too few answers. As a consequence, those in the middle may not get around to doing something to correct a social problem because it is not yet a problem to them. Experiencing a problem can make it *their* problem. There is a name for it—"social learning"—and for some it is the eye opener they need to get off the sidelines.[45] Although many people think that making a commitment to some specified action comes first, they frequently overlook that commitment is often developed *through action*. The emotion and memory of what they experience can provide the necessary motivation to put aside *the thinking* and to start *the doing*.

Reading about the statistics of a problem rarely moves us as much as experiencing the statistics. The core of many self-organizing efforts is made up of those who have *experienced* a particular social problem. Their obesity or the obesity of those in their family or among their friends is more than enough reason for doing something they literally live with. Or a teenager they know has given up on his or her education by dropping out and hanging out or getting pregnant, and they can see how much young people forfeit when they give up on themselves. Seeing someone trying to live on the street or under a bridge may also be enough to prompt action. It is one thing to read about such problems, but to experience them, one way or another, is often the necessary emotional prod that gets people involved. A core group looking for enough others to join them will not so much seek to persuade others there is a problem, but instead find ways that others can experience the problem, which has the potential of powerfully persuading. The social problem may be near at hand but out of sight. Leave it to the core group to make more visible the problem others have neglected but now cannot avoid.

Along with getting others to experience a social problem, a core group may also employ the rhetoric of crisis. "Crisis" denotes immediacy and, although such rhetoric can be overdone, it does get others' attention. Without a crisis the urgency of doing something about a problem may be harder to summon. Obviously, a crisis may be mostly in the eye of the beholder, but often that extra descriptive flourish gets attention paid and action underway.[46] On the positive side, a core group may also find ways for others to *experience the change* they want, not just the social problem they encounter. The visible example of a core group helping the homeless by sharing their resources and asking others to do the same makes social attention more than just a speech or pamphlet or blog talk. It engages those willing to join in, if only temporarily, to share not only resources but a mutual experience.

My discussion here should not oversimplify the wide variety of responses that a core group is likely to confront as it uses experiencing a social problem or experiencing a desired change in order to draw others in. The street entertainer does not hold everyone's attention who stops by—his songs or magic tricks will not please everyone. The crowded restaurant draws us in, but the menu may not be to our liking. That is one reason why a core group may maintain a certain amount of strategic ambiguity so that the widening circle of participants is not bound to just one objective, one desired outcome. Those at the core probably do not have a "master strategy"—they're too experienced for that. They know that "broad experimentation" works better to get others to join them who may have some ideas or actions of their own to contribute.[47]

(2) *Striving to solve the problem*: Another dynamic to enlarge the circle are the relationships that develop among those who strive together. The pleasure in the striving comes from the doing with others, not just the destination they strive for. There may be those who knew each other before the undertaking, which accounts for their coming together in the first place, but they are likely to encounter others they did not know before. A new experience of solidarity with what were once only strangers can make the undertaking all the more worthwhile. As a consequence, new generative relationships that grow out of the shared experience can be as important, upon reflection, as the undertaking itself. My experience in political campaigns is that strangers come together for a cause, a candidate, and end up finding each other. The finding and the relationships generated can become as important as the undertaking itself. As I noted earlier, whether it is a losing headquarters on election night or a winning headquarters, people are reluctant to give up the experience, the bonding they shared, regardless of the actual outcome.

Goal-minded activists often fail to understand that it is the collective *striving* for something, not just the something, that holds joiners to an undertaking. Striving, like making art, is about the process, the experience itself. Social attention and self-organizing can rescue those who welcome an escape from the humdrum of their daily routines. Those who gain satisfaction only from attaining their goal may be more easily discouraged, more distracted if the desired end is elusive or harder to achieve than expected. For those centered on striving, the journey itself is what counts regardless of what obstacles they encounter along the way. Striving also becomes a form of compensation for uncertainty—the uncertainty that a new social practice undertaken with others will, in fact, succeed.[48] Those in the core group, who know how important the very act of striving is, will try to link everyone's efforts together, no matter how fragmented they may seem, to make it harder for anyone to walk away with a shrug if she knows that she's letting others down and jeopardizing the chances of success.

(3) *Deputizing specific tasks*: Some people are perpetual joiners and get spread too thin; their interests wane and energies lapse. One antidote is to ask them to concentrate on just one thing at a time, what I call "deputization," by taking responsibility for a specific someone or a specific place in the community that may be vulnerable. It may be acting as a designated driver for someone who has had too much to drink, or taking on an assigned hour each day as part of a block watch to prevent crime, or adopting a specific section of highway where the litter needs attention. Not every social practice fits every size foot. Sometimes it means finding a specific task that fits well with a person's background and talents—not something that seems imposed and unnatural to perform. Some may especially prosper if their deputization becomes visible to others. They more than welcome the attention and recognition for whatever specific contribution they are trying to make.[49] Others may find that they feel better about themselves when, instead of comparing their performance to professionals', they discover "[t]he feeling that I did this myself, and it's good, [which] often beats the feeling that professionals did this for me and it's perfect."[50] Deputization can also mean giving those who were not part of a core group some influence of their own. Their input is solicited to help shape or steer where things should go. It may be hard for those who were there from the beginning to widen what was once an inner circle but, as I have already noted, leaving strategies unfinished or subject to amendment can open an undertaking to more, and perhaps better, ideas and directions.[51]

(4) *Offering lots of feedback—small wins and the prospects of success*: Feedback is essential when an undertaking is far-flung and those participating need to know what others like them are doing in order to keep things going. We are all familiar with the feedback of a fundraising

campaign that keeps in touch with us about what others have already contributed—how many and how much. Feedback is just common sense in letting everyone know that they are part of an undertaking gathering steam that needs their continued efforts. Feedback about whatever progress is being made, no matter how tenuous, can also have a contagious effect by drawing others to the undertaking who were waiting for some good news before joining in. Getting on a bandwagon is relatively easy. Anticipating larger numbers can help produce them. People come looking for the crowd they've heard about and in so doing swell the crowd. The exaggeration may be a kind of social placebo but it works for those who need it. After all, *no one* really knows what it will take to find enough others. Otherwise, if too many drift away, maintaining critical mass can be elusive or episodic as others see the tide going out to excuse their own withdrawal from an undertaking.

Forms of communication that reach those waiting to see what happens are essential. Communication deprives them of their well-worn excuses of "I didn't know," or "I hadn't heard." With so many ways these days of reaching those in social networks, membership associations, and public spaces, those excuses should no longer ring true. Every undertaking needs small wins that can be shared and broadcast to the public world. Small wins are markers along the way that help keep the social attention and self-organizing effort moving along. The prospects of success also have to be emphasized as nourishment for those who are not at all sure that success will be realized, which harks back to William James's observation that faith in a fact helps create the fact. I found my graduate students usually needed some modicum of success at one point or another in a class exercise or project to sustain their initial enthusiasm for it. Ironically, sometimes their mistaken assumptions about being successful in a class exercise were enough to keep them seriously in the game, so to speak. It didn't matter that they were mistaken; it provided motivation nonetheless. Enough others had to believe they could succeed.

Nothing, however, succeeds like success. An exhilaration comes from taking part in an undertaking that accomplishes, more or less, what it set out to do. This is especially true when few or no ties bound those who came together in the first place. The ties that develop, at least temporarily, are similar to what can happen in military campaigns, political insurgencies, walk-a-thons, or getting someone's car out of a snow bank. With a stranger's car stuck in that snow bank, those who stop to assist usually look for more help from others passing by to make the task easier and less time-consuming. No one really knows how many it will take to get the car out of the snow bank. All they know is the more down there helping, the more likely that together they'll succeed. And the longer they stay with the effort the less likely that anyone will withdraw or drift away. They have sunk costs in the effort they have already made together, which makes it harder for anyone to give up before enough others get the car out of the snow bank.[52]

A concluding cautionary note here. Success, strangely enough, can have its own problems. If a core group organizes carpools in an attempt to relieve traffic congestion, others, who stopped driving and took mass transit because of the congestion, may resume driving and bring back the congestion. If others manage to wage a successful water-conservation campaign, public authorities may be tempted to divert water to other more profligate areas, thus penalizing those for their thrift. If too many neighborhood crime watchers report suspicious activity to the police on 911, they may prevent those requiring emergency help from getting through. There is no guarantee that we can fix a social problem once and for all. Even if we succeed in getting it resolved, new and unforeseen problems are likely to intrude. Social problems are hard to solve.[53]

CHAPTER 4

And Here Come the Boomers

Finding enough others to bring about social change is not easily done. We know that and it accounts for the modest undertakings some of us pursue, and for some it accounts for not making any effort of their own. The Boomer generation, however, may be exceptional in overcoming such a lackluster choice given their upbringing, which encouraged them to think that they were special and that they could accomplish anything they put their mind to. The early Boomers, born between 1946 and 1955, were in the forefront of the social and political turmoil of the 1960s. The social change of the 1970s followed close behind as early Boomers and late Boomers, those born between 1956 and 1964, liberated themselves from established norms, which fit well their sense of being special and entitled.

Their liberated moments, however, did not last long. Jackson Lears noted perceptively in *No Place of Grace* that when social movements have been rooted in loyalties beyond self, they were far more effective than "when they succumbed to the dominant ethos of individual fulfillment" and "lost moral force and faltered."[1] This seemed true of those Boomers who stepped forward in the 1960s to take on a range of social problems only to fade later when they went their separate ways. As I once observed, they acted out their discontent with "the system without giving much thought to what should take its place, and eventually the great majority made their peace and found their place in the established order." Their public lives of protest moved on to private lives full of therapies and consumables within the system that had indulged them but would not finally yield.[2] Many were tagged as "yuppies," young urban professionals, as they found a place for themselves within the system, but with professional credentials now giving them standing and reinforcing their sense of being special. Not all those who chose the professional road, however, traveled to the same place. For some, what started as a quarrel with established institutions in the 1960s was sustained in their public interest work, the helping professions, and the movement for workplace democracy, among others.

I have always envied the Boomers' numbers. When they sneeze, we are all likely to catch a cold. I know that much has been said and written to disabuse us of the notion that the Boomers are a homogeneous group, and I don't want to fall into that careless assumption when referring to them as "enough others." Of course their numbers are impressive, but no one can manipulate an entire generation into having an easily discernible and common mind-set. When they were young, the Boomers, as all generations do, identified with each other as they experienced the same fads, events, and attention of others. When they became adults that self-conscious generational phase receded as they went their own ways into marriages, jobs, and far-flung communities, fragmenting the shared identity of their growing-up years. Self-realization and self-improvement have been watchwords for them ever since.

Now this aging Boomer generation comes to a new chapter in their lives. Will they remain preoccupied with looking out for number one as best they can in an uncertain age of government retrenchment? The threats to their Medicare and Social Security benefits are serious. It's understandable that all of them will want to make a soft landing in retirement, a retirement they will try to avoid as long as they can and the cost of which they would rather not confront. The aging Boomer generation, like at every other phase of their lives, will not go unnoticed. Seventy-nine million of them represent 26 percent of our country's population. Think of it—between 2011 and 2030, 10,000 Boomers *every day* will cross the threshold of 65.[3] Characteristic of their generation, however, Boomers are far from accepting decline and old age as a given. They have not forgotten their specialness and will, no doubt, resist the moniker of "elderly." They maintain an attitude of almost naïve defiance toward what others before them have accepted, and certainly old age will become newly contested ground. We cannot yet know what Boomers will make of their defiance, but it provides some basis for hoping that they will use their numbers and their later years to renew some of the restless energy that once characterized their young, evolving story in the 60s and 70s.

You can tell that my perspective on the Boomers does not come from being one of them. I have always been a few years ahead of them but have always looked back at their approaching herd. As I've already noted, storytelling is a very imprecise art and the distinctions I make here are highlights, not details, of our respective generational journeys. Nonetheless, highlights always bear some crude truths. I remember that the schools I attended when growing up always added a new wing soon after my graduation, evidence of a school system anticipating the approach of Boomers close behind. As I was growing up, war for me meant World War II and its victory over evil. War for the Boomers meant Vietnam and, for many, deserved their scorn. My young generation in the 1950s was once tagged with being "silent." The young Boomers were anything but silent in the 1960s. Although many Boomers served in Vietnam, their generation was publicly marked more by their protests than their service. In the mid-60s, I served as an artillery officer on the West German border, the 5K zone between East and West, and I remember my concern about having my tour of duty extended by President Johnson as the Vietnam War became a larger and prolonged conflict. The extension never came. I did not question, but only feared, the need for it. Just five years later, I found myself traveling to Canada with Congressman Ed Koch to meet with Boomers who had gone there to avoid military service.

After a decade of government service, I moved on to graduate school teaching, which brought me together with many students of the Boomer generation, and I learned a great deal about where they came from and where they were going. For the decade of the 1980s, I worked with both early and late Boomers in my classrooms—a contingent that sought to shape distinctive lifestyles for themselves. Most of them sought the status that came with a graduate school credential, but I also wanted them to learn or relearn what it meant to achieve something together that none of them could possess alone. I wanted them to become a different kind of professional who worked *with* their clientele, not just *for* them. I didn't want them to just nestle in the security of the existing order unprepared to change the status quo. It left too much out of what they could offer. As graduate students, their most urgent question was "what should I know?" I also wanted to address their concern of "how should I live?" It was not a vocational question but an intellectual and moral one. In professional fields staked out with "no trespassing" signs, I wanted them to be gentle intruders. After all, professionalism has come to mean little more than being good enough at what you do to get paid for it.

It can, however, mean much more. I wanted them to offer themselves, not just their credentials, and to use their moral imagination to determine where they were most needed. Now that they have traveled their respective roads to status and a modicum of success, they, along with other members of their generation, perhaps can once again and freshly ask "where am I most needed?" Their ongoing stories remain so central in this new century because of their sheer numbers. It is why the Boomers no doubt still constitute enough others to make a substantial difference in how they might, how we might, address our mutual social problems.

Why now? Why them? Simply because the Boomers are reaching a stage of their lives that gives them the time and certainly the license—they have always claimed the license—to be the critical difference in establishing new social practices through self-organizing. Their social attention and numbers have always given them the potential to disrupt old ways of looking at events as they unfold, to pursue new ways of responding to events, and, more important, to shape the trajectory of those events with something of their own making. If too many of them remain only preoccupied with what government should do about *their* social problems, it is difficult to believe that the Boomer generation will be able to hold on to all the government benefits they expect through Medicare and Social Security. Although I don't expect that they will willingly give up what they have always expected government to provide, I do see the possibility that Boomers and all of us will do more for ourselves and others when it comes to health care, education, and welfare, if only to mitigate the enormous cost of expecting government to somehow do it for us. The costs for health care alone are squeezing what government can spend on education for the young. The federal government now spends $7 on the elderly for each $1 it spends on children.[4] It does not portend a rosy future for our country when economic decline might go hand in hand with trying to support an aging population at the expense of those children and young people who are our future. The Boomers themselves will be critical in reconciling the contradiction. I don't think it will require altruism on everyone's part but rather the recognition that to make do, we have to find ways of doing things differently—as the Boomers have so many times done in the past. Perhaps they will welcome making such distinctions that once again make them a special generation in their own eyes and the eyes of others.

I have always quarreled, as have behavioral economists, with the calculation that rational self-interest and the economic models that exclude most other variables are predictive of how individuals and markets perform. I mention this here because I know some will shake their heads doubting that we can expect a greater sharing of human and material resources with others. I disagree. Those who think individual behavior is only driven by what an individual calculates is in his or her best interest ignore the possibility that the greater sharing of resources is quite conceivable if Boomers' self-interest is served *and* they also find ways to do their part in maintaining a social safety net. The rational self-interest school often misses that we are rarely just autonomous citizens but interdependent and empathetic. My earlier discussion of self-organizing from local practices to social movements offers clear evidence of that. Our history does not support the rather cramped models of self-interested behavior which are of use in some limited economic contexts but are inadequate to explain or predict what we will do in a variety of complicated social contexts. Using fewer variables makes for elegant models but such models are unequal to the rich stew of possibilities that may arise from new or renewed social practices and the paths we forge with enough others.

Self-interest is rarely just a matter of what each of us wants. What we want can also bend to a social referendum of what others want for us and for themselves. Think of the anti-smoking story. The self-interest of those who smoked was clearly evident and yet their health and the health of those exposed to secondary smoke moved the country away from "do as you please" to "do what's good for you *and* those you live and work with." In 1964, 42 percent of Americans smoked. Change took awhile, but only 20 percent smoke now. The social attention directed at smokers didn't start with government, but, as social attitudes toward smoking changed, government also had to respond as it did by banning cigarette commercials on TV, requiring health warnings on cigarette packs, and imposing higher taxes when those packs were sold. With smoking prohibited in many indoor spaces, once acceptable behavior was outlawed.

The self-interests of a Boomer generation will likely undergo serious reexamination given the unavoidable circumstance of their aging and newly imposed limits on government spending. As a consequence, they may very well look for new ways to deal with the social problems of health care, education, and the needs of those less fortunate. The narrative ground, what Boomers inherited, and the liberal ground, what Boomers created free of any inheritance, is a distinction that many of them clearly made as young adults when rejecting some of the values they grew up with in favor of new practices that were partly their own creation. I think their liberal ground may once again assert itself as aging

Boomers create new social practices to meet existing social problems—to render health care beyond the doctor's office, to educate young people beyond the school zone, and to pool their resources, in new and different ways, for those without. It may very well take the Boomers' numbers to launch such social practices beyond the parochial efforts already being made. Their numbers are likely to make a real difference—always their numbers.

Health Care beyond the Doctor's Office

As everyone knows, the high costs of health care have become an enormously complicated and contentious social problem. What should government do? What should government not do? It is an open sore in the body politic with politicians, experts, and the 24/7 media all having plenty to say about it. Such contention is not likely to end soon, if ever, but for the moment let's put aside what *they* say government should do or not do and look at what *we* can do in our families, neighborhoods, and communities to help contain costs. When it comes to health care and its costs, what a rich opportunity for aging Boomers to do more of looking after themselves and others. One cannot find a more urgent social problem that is bound up in their self-interests and everyone else's. The high cost of health care for an aging Boomer generation will soon become everyone's problem. New social practices, however, can help alleviate our health care bind not just for the Boomers' benefit but as common ways of contributing to the overall health of Americans of any age.

"Affordable health care," like so many popular phrases, sounds good but, in fact, is a social problem of the first order. It implies that whatever the medical establishment can do for us that is "affordable" should be done. It leaves out our failure to do more for ourselves and for others beyond the doctor's office thereby enlarging the concept of what health care really is. Affordable health care does not necessarily start with the medical establishment but starts with enough others looking out for those who need social attention, support, and advice. It may be our own extended family, or elderly shut-ins down the block or across town. It may be anyone in the workplace or wherever we find others whose health and habits might profit from our social attention, support, and advice. And, of course, it might be any one of us who also need to discover better ways of taking care of ourselves.[5] Simply put, many of our individual health problems are of our own making. Our failure to eat nutritious food and exercise regularly cannot be laid at the doorstep of government or the medical establishment. Although we will continue to seek medical attention for such problems, when we start eating better, exercising more, and getting others to do likewise, we become part of the answer, not just part of the problem. Affordable health care then becomes, in part, something of our own making.

My argument, however, doesn't exclude the essential role of the medical establishment in the delivery of professional health care. Part of the Affordable Health Care Act of 2010 supports the concept of a "patient-centered medical home" in the office of a primary care doctor based on a team approach using all of the doctor's supporting staff. The new law also gives each Medicare beneficiary an "annual wellness visit," which doesn't require finding something wrong in order for the doctor to be paid. Nonetheless, good health depends as much or more on what we can do for ourselves and others as on what we can afford the medical establishment to do for us. At present, America has only 7,000 geriatricians to deal with the aging Boomer generation over the next 10 years.

Staring us in the face is the serious and alarming problem of obesity, which is hard to ignore when you see it in your own family or pass by a couple or whole family who obviously need plenty of sidewalk room. Such folks weigh heavily on health care costs, and their condition is estimated to add $14 billion a year to the national bill. The obesity problem has many dimensions. For children alone, one estimate puts the obesity rate at 14 percent for 6- to 11-year-olds and 17 percent for adolescents, and it is estimated that over 70 percent of obese children will be obese adults "with increased risks of diabetes, heart disease, and certain cancers."[6] Excessive weight gain in pregnancy has been identified as one serious contributor to the development of such diseases in later life.[7] We have known for some time that children from less affluent neighborhoods have the highest rates of obesity. Although some school systems are trying to reduce these rates, what these youngsters consume at home obviously lies beyond the schools' jurisdiction. That is why the problem cannot be solved just by government initiatives but by families and neighbors making their efforts too. Schools can limit bake sales and offer cooking classes and encourage more exercise during classroom breaks, but parents will also have to consider more nutritious dishes to serve and reinforce the cooking classes and exercises learned at school by practice at home.

Unlike the anti-smoking campaigns, anti-obesity campaigns are far more complicated and don't yield any simple solutions. Many professionals are concerned with and working on the obesity problem—specialists in psychology, agriculture economics, physical therapy, and on and on. They have no lack of ideas and experiments under way to chip away at the problem, but when such specialists see the underlying culture as recalcitrant, it brings the social problem back to us. "Preventable causes of death such as smoking, poor diet and physical inactivity, and misuse of alcohol have been estimated to be responsible for 900,000 deaths annually—nearly 40% of total yearly mortality in the U.S."[8] The professionals most engaged with the obesity problem are, of course, family physicians who see the consequences of obesity every day. Some write prescriptions for the healthy food they want their patients to eat more of and direct them to local farmer's markets.[9]

Government is no bystander either. The Obama administration with Michelle Obama at the forefront put in place the Healthy Hunger-Free Kids Act that helps provide more nutritious school meals which Michelle has linked to her "Let's Move" campaign addressing childhood obesity. One of the major parts of the act is setting up and supporting local farm-to-school networks in order to provide fresh local foods for use in school meals.[10] Some mock such government intrusion thinking it's none of government's business, but it's everyone's business when the rising costs of health care affect all of us. What's wrong with the government's dietary advice to eat more fruits and vegetables but eat less of processed food with sodium, fat, and sugar?[11] What is not in dispute is that the health costs of those who are obese are 72 percent more than those of normal weight.[12] What the conservative media folk have right is that it's primarily our business. What they get wrong is that we are somehow doing enough about it. We couldn't be when with two-thirds of Americans are overweight.

Taking better care of ourselves and others means more than just doctor prescriptions and White House campaigns. Anti-obesity campaigns and new social practices are doable, but only if we change our cultural attitudes about which foods are good for us and which are not. That culture change won't come from government or talking heads. It will require enough others who change their eating and exercise habits. It will require enough others' rejection of what too many fast food outlets and grocery stores serve and sell us. Have you noticed that eating less especially becomes a problem when eating out? The humongous portions make you want to clean your plate if only to get your money's worth, but the portions are served on plates big enough to go sledding on.

Putting aside what we eat for the moment, what about exercise? On any given day, nearly 40 percent of Americans don't exercise at all.

We are what we eat, but we are also what exercise we manage to do. Walking when we can, driving when we must might be a useful adjustment to consider. Ah, but there are so many reasons why so many don't walk, much less engage in sports, gym classes, and other organized physical activities. Exercise takes time, certainly walking does, and so many Americans have become time-obsessed what with all there is to do in balancing work, family, and couch potato entertainment. I am often struck on my daily walks by how few are out doing the same. Many cars drive by and we wave to each other, but they are gone in a flash. Time is precious, habits are fixed, and walking seems so, well, slow. In many communities exercise has a place with bike paths and walking trails, but unless there is a supportive culture of outdoor activists, those paths and trails are usually not used with any regularity. In a few cities walking is less a pastime than a necessity. "Studies have shown that urban dwellers who walk or bike or take transit, instead of sitting behind the wheel of a car for every errand and commute to work, aren't as heavy as their suburban counterparts."[13]

It might also help if we considered turning off the TV. One good reason for couch potato citizens to get up and get out is eluding the seduction of commercials that offer in the most entertaining ways more salt and more sugar. Obesity is not just encouraged by sitting around too much, but also by commercials that invite us to imbibe, to enjoy, to relax, to be good to ourselves ("you owe it to yourself"). Junk food, however, offers no more nourishment than junk news. Furthermore, most marketing to children, who are rabid TV watchers, is for snack food, fast foods, sugary sodas, and cereals. They may not be couch potato citizens yet, but they are being groomed. Children aged 8–12 see on average 21 food ads a day, 7,600 a year. Half the ad time on children's shows is for food.[14]

One undertaking within most everyone's reach is home cooking, which unfortunately has declined as couples and families find faster ways to get their daily intake of food. This is especially true of those on the margins or living in poverty as they try to hold down multiple jobs and eat on the run.[15] Such work schedules also mean they have less time for workouts and exercise. Faster ways to eat often mean fast food and the extra calories that go with it. A culture change will be a tough slog. It won't be easy to drive by the takeout. For many Americans, meals are no longer occasions for enjoying what someone has prepared at home. Instead, prepackaged meals become supplements for watching TV, or eating in the car while going off somewhere, or children in their room munching away. Cooking for ourselves or family could certainly focus the mind on what we're eating and the ingredients involved. The very time and attention that cooking requires might educate or reeducate us about what is worthwhile to eat. When I look at what I spend on fresh produce as compared to the packaged stuff, I know that cost is not the primary reason for those who prefer the added sweetness and sodium that seduce their taste buds. And what about expanding home gardens, growing more of our own food, much as Michelle Obama is doing in her own garden on the South Lawn of the White House grounds?[16] "A 2003 study by a group of Harvard economists . . . found that the rise of food preparation outside the home could explain most of the increase in obesity in America." Does this account for the United States spending twice as much on health care per person than most European countries? Michael Pollan, quoting the study, thinks so. Pollan has done more than anyone to focus attention on the linkage between agribusiness and bad eating habits. Mass production, rather than home cooking, has increased our appetite for, and consumption of, all those goodies that are not good for us. For Pollan, "The path to a diet of fresher, unprocessed food . . . passes straight through the home kitchen."[17] It won't be easy to turn the ship around. Pollan says, "There's a lot of money to be made selling fast food and then treating the disease that fast food causes. One of the leading products of the American food industry has become patients for the American health care industry."[18]

So it brings me back to affordable health care. Whether or not you or I are obese, we pay indirectly for those who are. As their weight increases so do our costs. Some would argue that only the government can take on the agribusiness food industry and its major role in contributing to the obesity problem and that only government can get the health care industry to focus more on the prevention of chronic conditions and diseases. Perhaps incentives in the landmark Affordable Health Care Act of 2010 will get the health care industry to take on agribusiness, to reduce the consequences and insurance costs linked to obesity. Considering that the federal government spends nearly $150 billion yearly on obesity-related conditions like diabetes, heart disease, and cancer, it makes sense that whatever government incentives are available would certainly help advance whatever culture change is possible. It's not an either/or proposition of what we do or what government does. It will take an array of initiatives, both private and public, to make a real difference. Only one in five now smoke but one in three are obese—exercise alone is certainly not enough, just as nutrition is not enough. Just imagine, however, if the combination could reduce the obesity rate to one in five. Will it take

40 years to change the culture as it did in putting those who smoke outside? Can we afford in dollars and cents to wait that long?

Unnecessary health care presents another costly social problem. It is estimated that the amount of medical care that is unnecessary ranges from 10 to 30 percent.[19] If we could curb escalating health costs by doing more to look after each other, it would be a vital supplement to what the government and medical establishment try to do for us. Health care costs account for 15 percent of GDP and will likely escalate substantially with the Boomers aging each year.[20] The looming cost of supporting the aging Boomers makes them a big part of the social problem as well as a big part of the social answer. The aging Boomer generation is a mix of political attitudes, but one thing they seem to agree on is that adequate health care is their right, which implies that somehow with government support such care should be available. Their numbers are bound to add to health care spending, which is already $2.5 trillion a year, and if unchecked, the overuse of medical care will undoubtedly lead to various forms of rationing to cope with demand, unless demand is dealt with by a culture change. Provisions of the Affordable Health Care Act largely neglected to counter the *overuse* of our health care system. Pilot programs embedded in the act may move doctors to provide better care at less cost, but a culture change won't come from legislation alone. Rather it will come from a realization on our part that we can't have, can't afford all the medical services we may think we should have. The aging Boomer generation may be the first to face this realization and the first with the numbers to do something about it through self-organizing and new social practices. The right they claim to adequate health care may take their giving as well as their getting.[21]

The need for a culture change, which leads us to do more for ourselves and others beyond what the medical establishment can do for us, will also have to confront the culture of the medical establishment. That culture seeks to do more, not less, for us with office visits and prescriptions. As one commentator noted, "that's how doctors make money and that's how they protect themselves from lawsuits."[22] "Talk to your doctor" is the common line offered by pharmaceutical companies before trying their products. "Talk to your doctor" is what professional therapists and medical technicians also tell us to do as a check against their advice or test findings. "Talk to your doctor," however, usually involves an office visit to be squeezed in with a raft of appointments that primary care physicians have to juggle most every day. Their medical practice is bound by limits of time, paperwork demands, and their own expertise.

Not only is their time precious, their numbers are falling behind the demand for their advice. A 2009 report of the Association of American Medical Colleges projects a shortage of 150,000 primary care doctors by 2025.[23] As professionals they are already overwhelmed by those seeking their care with their daily practice becoming less hierarchical, if not by choice, then by necessity. Since only so many patients can "talk to their doctor" on any given day, nurses and paraprofessionals are assuming more responsibility. An annual checkup can often last not more than 15–20 minutes, and when my wife and I want to talk with our physician, we prepare detailed notes and all but rehearse our questions before seeing him in order to make efficient use of his limited time for us. Fortunately, over the years he has encouraged us to do what we can for ourselves in maintaining good health, and that is what all of us will be doing more of, like it or not, given the shortage of primary care doctors.

If more of us educate ourselves rather than rely exclusively on "talking to the doctor," we may find that we have more discretion in how we take care of ourselves than we thought. Consider the cost and return of various screenings such as mammograms to detect breast cancer in women and tests for prostate cancer in men. Some would leave it to the medical establishment whether to screen or not. We may feel incompetent to make such a choice and defer to the experience and judgment of doctors, but it doesn't keep us from learning more about false positives that occur often in mammograms or that, in later age, detecting a slow-growing cancer in the prostate does not necessarily require any serious remedial measures. We should, at least, understand that the professional thoroughness of medical practitioners is also tied to their getting paid for testing and avoiding the risk of being sued for malpractice for failing to test.

Prescription drugs, which account for 10 cents of every dollar spent on health care, is another area where we can educate ourselves rather than merely being consumers alerted daily by the substantial drug advertising on TV advising us to "talk to your doctor." Doctors can write prescriptions quickly, which saves them time, and we may go off to a pharmacy without further thought as to whether we really need what the TV commercial trumpeted and the doctor prescribed. Many of us may be skeptical of alternative health remedies, but the very fact that we may consider them shows that, if we want to, we are capable of educating ourselves. For those who don't take time to educate themselves, there is the opportunity for family, friends, and coworkers to help educate them. Now, of course, "we are not doctors, but . . ." our experience and a careful reading of drug side effects may be of real value to others.

Second opinions have also been greatly enlarged by online Google searches and sharing information via crowd sourcing.[24] Our medical data is kept private by those who have it—doctors, hospitals, insurance companies—but that doesn't mean we can't voluntarily share it with others if we so choose. There are many online health information initiatives and though one person's participation in furnishing his or her medical data seems trivial, if enough others contribute, it could add up to substantial advances in medical research and its applications.[25] Such personal information can come back to us in aggregate form that gives us more to go on than just heading to the doctor's office for more tests. Organizing wellness festivals is another option beyond the doctor's office. Where we lived in New Hampshire, the local Rotary Club organized such an annual festival for a Saturday in September. The centerpiece was to get residents to come downtown to get free blood pressure, cholesterol, skin, oral health, and hearing tests. Nutrition measures were also shared. Soup and bread makers were invited to take part. From the money raised at the wellness festival, a "Healthy Me" program was started with the provision of healthy afterschool snacks seeking to help local children, one-third who are overweight or obese.

When preventive medicine fails, becoming ill means going to bed or sometimes going to the hospital for medical attention. Many of those who suffer from chronic conditions, however, occupy a middle ground requiring the attention of others from day to day but not necessarily the medical establishment. It has been estimated that 90 million Americans, 25 percent of the population, suffer from chronic conditions that last for years and years.[26] How we attend to such a large cohort poses a challenge for the medical establishment, but also for what family, friends, and neighbors can do. Our care and support can make an enormous difference for those who need social attention that helps them bear their suffering and can also help relieve it. There are so many ailments and afflictions in old age that may not require admission to health care facilities but still require social attention—helping those who suffer falls with strengthening their balance and dealing with their fears of falling again, helping those who need exercises for bladder incontinence, or visiting those who just want company to fight off depression. For such folks, much can be done without their having to resort to more prescription drugs or institutionalization. With more limits on government support likely coming in the years ahead, more of us may need to extend caregiving to those beyond immediate family who are homebound and need attention and companionship.[27]

Social attention can also be extended to those in assisted living and continuing care facilities nearby. Yes, there are tasks that only trained staff can perform, but there are many hours of the day when residents and patients can benefit from those with time and talents to share. My wife, Alice, spends two hours each Monday and Friday morning with several wheelchair-bound residents in the medical center of a continuing care facility nearby where we live. Alice shares maps, stories, handcrafts, and other topics for those who have little else to command their daily attention except TV and meals. She has learned to fill their silences but also to listen to what they have to say when they want to do the talking. Age often needs companionship from those of comparable years. There is an acceptance and understanding when the elderly can share similar memories and experiences. Social attention goes beyond what the medical establishment and technology can offer. And far from such social attention being only of value to those bed-ridden or house-bound, research shows that a caregiver's health can benefit as well from making the social connection. For the past 20 years, my wife has suffered from nerve pain and dysthymia, a mild form of chronic anxiety and depression. With medication Alice was able to resume her teaching career, but there have been times since leaving such work that she has experienced episodes of anxiety and depression. As her husband I have tried to compensate in various ways for the daily burden she has faced, but recently the social attention that she has brought to others and they to her at the continuing care facility where she volunteers has made an enormous difference. The cost of her medication remains substantial, but the social network in which she flourishes is priceless. Individual health problems are also social problems with social-support answers that can be something of our own making.[28] What aging Boomers might do for themselves and for others in pursuing old and new health practices beyond the doctor's office could be as revolutionary as anything they did together in the tumultuous 1960s and 1970s.

Education Beyond the School Zone

My friend, Larry Cremin, once the preeminent historian of American education, saw schools and colleges as only one educative source in the story of American education, which he chronicled in a three-volume history. Unfortunately, since Larry's untimely death in 1990, his work has been eclipsed by those who, as one former Cremin student and colleague put it, "deal with education as if it is a synonym for schooling . . . as if one cannot imagine anything that educates without somehow equating it with schooling."[29] For Cremin, education "went on anywhere and everywhere, not only in schoolrooms, but in kitchens, manses, churches, meetinghouses, sheds erected in fields, and shops erected in towns; that pupils were taught by anyone and everyone, not only by schoolmasters, but by parents, tutors, clergymen, lay readers . . . physicians, lawyers, artisans and shopkeepers."[30] In fact, Noah Webster's 1828 dictionary did not even mention schooling in the definition of "educate."[31] In all his work, Larry Cremin argued convincingly that the variety of educational institutions and educators in America's far-flung communities, what he called "the ecology of education," has been a rich and enduring source of education beyond the local school zone. For Cremin, the "deliberate nurture" of others' development is at the heart of what educators do. I told him on one occasion that, given his theory of education, "we are all potential educators." So who are the community educators among us whose curricula and classrooms lie beyond the local school zone? They are indeed significant others—ministers, priests, rabbis, librarians, curators, grant makers, local history buffs, public television and print journalists, pro bono lawyers and paralegals, public health and day care staff, business trainers and employers, peer and youth group counselors, adult literacy and workshop instructors, self-help and community organizers, and all manner of voluntary associations, their leaders, and their websites.

Public schools, which are an extension of both local and state governments, obviously play the central role in educating young people, and yet there are so many others who contribute or can contribute to their learning. One would assume that education begins in the home. We know, however, that for many reasons parents leave more and more of what they think of as education to the schools and perhaps accidentally to the ubiquitous educative influence of television.[32] In many homes, young people are left to their own designs and the distractions of TV and websites—much the same as what their couch potato parents indulge in. Few demands, little education, just entertainment. As Cremin so vividly documented, it has not always been so, but in this day and age with two parents working or single parents with their own disadvantages, the quarrel is almost exclusively with what schools do or don't do. Where once parents prescribed their children's conduct and set the example for how they should engage in the public world, now many do neither. Both parents and schools usually focus on the deficiencies of young people—what they don't know, what they should learn. So if parents and schools are preoccupied with measuring student deficits through testing, there is plenty of room for community educators beyond the school zone to help develop those capacities of young people, which are not currently being attended to in school or the home setting. Failing students are not just those who drop out or those with poor test scores. Failing students are also those who are not adequately prepared for citizenship beyond the couch potato variety.

The community educators I have met have many different agendas—public safety, public health, the arts, environmental protection, job training, and on and on, but they can also be purposeful in nurturing the development of young people's social attention and their skills of learning to problem solve with others—an education that prepares them for active citizenship and democratic self-rule. Such learning can be the subtext of almost any community organization or initiative engaging young people's interests and energies. For example, community educators can help young people form their own circles—democratic circles—to help them learn to shape their own answers and choices when together they identify problems, frame them, and decide how to proceed. There is no hierarchy in a circle and those in a circle cannot turn their backs on anyone who is part of it. When looking at a circle, where does it begin or where does it end? In this way, young people discover their capacities and the capacities of others rather than just being the recipients of someone's services. Unfortunately, this is not a lesson that most formal schooling offers or encourages. Many teachers resist creating democratic circles in their classrooms for fear of losing control. They take for granted that what they know and want to convey is far superior to what they think students know. They too often neglect the educator role, preferring the more limited role of delivering information and some knowledge off the shelf that their students can use for test-taking.

Let me share here what my students learned in the democratic circles we organized inside and outside the classroom. The easy part was telling others about the personal experiences they brought along with them as a form of introduction. For many, the harder part was learning to get out of themselves. There is a word for such decentering, "allocentric," which means to have "one's interest and attention centered on other persons." Making such a shift was important because they came to learn far more than just being content with their own stories and opinions. An ego trip took them nowhere except to places they already knew. Instead, they discovered the art of putting themselves in someone else's shoes. It started with listening—really listening—to what others had to say. For a student to merely say "If I were you" missed the point. Such advice was just a polite way of advancing his own opinion instead of trying to see the matter from different points of view. That was not putting himself in the other people's shoes; that was putting them in his. Some commentators think that such *deliberation* as a practice is withering, especially among young people, as a result of the new efficiency of solo online searching for information and opinion. Others think that online anonymity can encourage candor and that is good for deliberation. But more than candor is required in democratic circles. I think young people are likely to find that learning to listen, frame problems, and deliberate with others are skills far more nuanced than that. My students certainly did, and I will have more to say about deliberation in the next chapter.

What about those who find it hard to think of themselves as community educators? There is the obvious role of being mentors. Leaving mentoring to professionals is not adequate. There are simply not enough of them. Mentoring is something we all can do. Mentoring is a gift but not all gifts are the same. Some mentors give advice, others critique performance, and still others open doors of opportunity. Mentoring is sometimes offered unconditionally, but more often than not, a mentor acts like an educator who expects that the young person being helped has to do certain things if the relationship is to be sustained. There is a social linkage. Malcolm Gladwell has written about the social linkages that contribute to a young person's later success and the consequences when those linkages don't exist. "They lacked something that could have been given to them . . . a community around them that prepared them properly for the world." Gladwell calls this "squandered talent."[33]

There are so many ways to help young people find their way out of the dead ends that too many confront. We don't talk about apprenticeships much anymore, but we do know about internships—a relatively easy and inexpensive way to include those not ready or qualified for paid jobs. And there are community brokers who can help put young people together with those offering internships as well as nonprofit organizations that do a host of other things for them. For example, Oasis Community Impact in East Nashville, Tennessee, developed youth mobilizing where young people research social problems such as predatory lending, fast tax schemes, and identity theft.[34] Or consider what Wendy Wheeler is doing at the Innovation Center, a national intermediary organization, which, among many other initiatives, is working with youth leaders in New Haven, Connecticut, through the YMCA and the Hill Youth Action team focused on gang violence and teen pregnancy prevention.[35] And in the community where my wife and I now live, there are 115 volunteer mentors involved with mental health counseling and parenting classes for fathers along with a teen pregnancy prevention effort at the high school.[36] School dropouts pose a serious challenge for any community seeking to recover their wasted or lost potential, with young female dropouts many times more likely to become single mothers with no help from boyfriends who have little means to support the children they father.

And it is not just the K–12 ages that need more social attention. I think of Wick Sloane, a Boomer who once studied with me and who is now trying so hard to rescue the squandered talent of young adults in a midnight class of expository writing at Bunker Hill Community College in Boston. How did he get there, and why does he care? When I asked him recently, he said that for his students to be able to write a "simple declarative sentence can show that their voice can count in the world." Wick was drawn to Bunker Hill because he saw the challenge of helping students become solid members of society, able to act as citizens and able to land a real job. And, according to Wick, "that ain't easy!" His students have had some serious distractions. "Every semester I deal with shootings." One student told him, "I didn't finish my homework because my son was shot. He's OK now." Another explained, "I'm sorry I missed class. My boyfriend was murdered." Wick is sure that the great majority of Bunker Hill students have an intellect "equal to mine or yours," but "too much of their energy" has gone to "survival rather than education." Wick wants to find money for them in the form of grants that would pay students $10 an hour for studying in designated rooms at Bunker Hill and in public libraries using ID cards they could swipe and then get paid the following week. That is certainly thinking outside the box for a Boomer who was raised and educated safely within the box of elite schooling at Exeter, Williams, and Yale. Years back, however, Wick sent his daughter to a public school in West Hartford and found the school had no expectations for anyone. So he ran for school board, won, and made sure the board hired a new superintendent tied to a performance contract. Then Wick was off to Hawaii's higher education system as CFO and discovered the "astonishing motivation" of students at a community college. Returning to Boston, Wick headed for Bunker Hill.[37] There are many ways that Boomers and all of us can make a difference as educators and mentors.

Pooling Resources

Boomers are not likely to let go of their role as avid consumers. They long ago made their peace with a market-driven economy and its reliance on consumption for the economic well-being of the country. But the Boomers, like many others caught between their consumer desires and what they can afford after the mortgage and credit crunch of recent years, may find new reasons in their aging to reexamine what they actually need as compared to what they still would like to have. The Boomers' overall history may lead some of them to provide an example of sharing what they already have with those who have far less, especially if the fiscal condition of government—local, state, and federal—cannot sustain substantial social spending for the needs of those less fortunate. Impossible? Not really. If governments are limited in their spending due to massive deficits, then such a circumstance may provide the forceful shove for at least some of us to consider a greater sharing of what private wealth we have. It will take the example of enough others to make a real difference, and the Boomers will be prime candidates given their numbers. As an older set they may not have everything they want and rightly fear losing some of what they already have, but they do have substantial time, education, and possessions, which constitute a deep reserve of resources to share if they so choose. To paraphrase John Rawls, each of us is born into social circumstances not of our own doing. There is nothing just or unjust about such circumstance. What is just or unjust is whether the haves attend to or ignore the have-nots.[38]

A sign atop a large box in the lobby of a local bank invites canned food contributions: "You can, we can with one can. One item may not seem like a lot but when added together the sum will feed many. Deposit your items here each week." A simple idea, multiplying loaves and fishes so those in need can share in the plentitude of those with more than they need. It is what Parker Palmer aptly noted as "the illusion of scarcity v. the reality of abundance."[39] It would seem self-evident in most any community that there is plenty to go around if there are enough others to make it so. Unfortunately, too many "Lone Ranger" Americans still believe that everyone should stand on their own while too many couch potato citizens with a softer edge, but with better things to do, leave it to government to look after those in need. My quarrel is not with those who have so much per se but with those who have so much excess and fail to share it with those who don't. As my mother would say, "such a waste," which brings me back to the remarkable example of City Harvest in New York City noted in chapter 2.

City Harvest has become a very large undertaking since its beginnings in the early 1980s—a bottom-up effort of citizens who saw a great need and perfectly good food going to waste day after day after day. The assumption has always been that there is enough food in New York City to feed everyone if only enough others pool their resources. City Harvest takes the potential waste of food from restaurants, caterers, bakeries, hotels, coffee bars—you name it—and delivers it in a timely manner to those who might otherwise go without. City Harvest identifies key neighborhoods in the city where it focuses its resources. When a Fancy Food Show closed at the Javits Convention Center, 250 volunteers rescued enough food from the show to fill six trailers that then traveled to soup kitchens and food pantries across the city. City Harvest not only picks up wholesale, so to speak, from a wide variety of food outlets, it will pick up retail from individual New Yorkers who have more than 50 pounds of shelf-stable food. In addition, City Harvest has made the vital connection between healthy foods and good health. Its Healthy Neighborhoods outreach works with local community partners to provide outlets for nutritious food families can prepare as well as boost the neighborhood demand for such foods. Pooling resources becomes then not just an emergency effort to stave off hunger but a tool for promoting good eating habits.

Every spring, City Harvest conducts a Skip Lunch Fight Hunger campaign that takes what someone's lunch would otherwise cost and pools the proceeds for the healthy feeding of more than 20,000 kids and their families for an entire summer. City Harvest also rescues fresh produce from greenmarkets every summer—arugula, sweet corn, radishes, peaches, spinach, broccoli, zucchini, eggplant, and carrots. There is no end to the variety of initiatives City Harvest uses to channel the food abundance of New York City to those without it. Their example ripples out in so many ways—schoolchildren making hundreds of peanut butter and jelly sandwiches and walking them to a nearby center for the homeless; an emergency street fleet team of volunteers picking up small donations of perishable foods that would otherwise go a-wasting; a volunteer walking leftover sandwiches from Au Bon Pain to a community program not far away.

The aftershocks felt from the deep recession of 2008 produced even more demand for City Harvest's help. As intermediary social agencies found their dollar resources diminished, City Harvest's pooling of food stocks became an important resource for such agencies. When you know that enough food exists to feed everyone—the more than one million New Yorkers who otherwise go hungry—it becomes imperative to keep delivering more than 27 million pounds of food a year to support 600 agencies that feed people in need throughout the five boroughs of the city. And, most striking, it's *surplus* food. They're not robbing Peter to pay Paul. City Harvest is rescuing what otherwise might be wasted and sharing with those who have no such margin. And there are enough others to make it work. Just think if each community, big and small, wherever and however, pooled its food resources. The social problems of hunger and malnutrition would be greatly diminished and it could be something of our own making. Since the mid-1970s per capita food waste in the United States has increased by 50 percent. It is estimated that "we now throw away 40 percent of all the edible food produced."[40] Let each community estimate the need and the potential resources available to meet such need. Where such resources exist and only require that they be pooled and distributed, all it takes is some self-organizing to provide a food network to get the job done. Just ask City Harvest.[41]

Pooling resources of every kind is not a new social practice but surely one that could be greatly expanded to every corner of our country and led by aging Boomers whose relative abundance of food, clothes, furniture—you name it—could be organized, deployed, and shared. It doesn't necessarily mean going door to door collecting what would otherwise go to waste or stay stuffed in some closet, basement, attic, or garage, but it does mean organizing collection points, expanding recycling centers, and getting the word out so that traffic comes in and traffic goes out at such places for everyone interested in helping and everyone in need of help.[42] Why do I stress the potential of parochial efforts over larger regional and national anti-poverty policies and programs? Although funding to support such programs is always needed, our enormous, untapped, local resources not yet calculated, not yet pooled, may be especially important as governments tighten their belts. What is ironic is that our national economic recovery from the devastating 2008 recession is measured, in part, by our increasing consumption that "lumps necessities and luxuries together."[43] Not measured are the things you and I buy that others truly need for their own personal recovery but do not have the means to buy. That is where pooling what the haves have for sharing with the have-nots becomes more than a charitable gesture. It is a means for human recovery too often neglected in measuring our national well-being.

Obviously, it is not just surplus food that can be rescued. Unworn clothes, too, are a resource that can be pooled. Consider the New York Clothing Bank that occupies a 20,000-square-foot warehouse on the Brooklyn waterfront to which clothing manufacturers and retailers donate $10 million of their goods annually. Such new clothing is then distributed to nonprofit groups, which in turn reach out to 80,000 New Yorkers in need.[44] Most pooling obviously can't be on the scale of New York City, but it can work wherever there are enough others to clear out that stuff in their closets. It won't necessarily be brand new but welcome anyway. There have always been established local agencies with nonprofit thrift shops that take in various forms of gently used merchandise, sell them, and use the proceeds in support of their particular social mission. It is one form of pooling resources that puts sale proceeds to good use, sometimes for those less fortunate, sometimes for schools in need of more financial help. Or consider the recycling of wedding and prom dresses. It doesn't sound like doing much for entrenched social problems unless you consider the high cost for those who must put out their limited funds so their daughter can go to the dance or come to the altar. Ten years ago, two enterprising students started to recycle formal dresses, which have amounted to 20,000 over the decade with volunteers helping in a group called Operation Fairy Dust.[45] In my closets there are no prom dresses, but I have many, many new shirts—gifts from my daughter every Christmas—which I really don't need but keep around so not to offend her. C'mon, David!

There are many ways for a community to share with those in need. Community gardens, which I have already mentioned, can raise healthy local produce for sharing with others. Vacant lots can sometimes be transformed into divided plots that accommodate various vegetables and fruits tended by various gardeners from the surrounding community, and such spaces can also serve as meeting and training grounds.[46] To help the homeless where we live now, cooked dinners are brought to the men's shelter every evening by those in the community. When so many government jurisdictions are having a hard time making ends meet, the homeless population faces even greater hardships. Where can extra help come from? Private social agencies, of course, but pooling the human resources of a community is another way to meet the needs of the homeless among us, whether giving them first-aid attention, food, or providing a warm and safe shelter. Pooling resources can also mean expanding car pool networks, especially where there are few other transportation options available beyond dense urban areas. Carpooling is not just for commuters but for linking up those who need a ride somewhere with those who are going in that direction or willing to. Townspeople where we used to live in rural New Hampshire have organized a volunteer driver program to help others get to appointments and events or run errands. For the elderly, such help can be very important in maintaining some form of independence, although for some elderly it is not always a matter of preserving their independence but, instead, creating welcoming places where they can experience togetherness and interdependence. Pooling their resources is not done for others but for themselves and stretches what each has by a common sharing in one residence. Shared housing programs usually operated by nonprofit organizations offer a new start for those left to fend for themselves—widows and widowers with no children or no children close by to look in or after them.

Think of all the books each of us has that we never read or will never read again. They can go to a local library but also to hospitals, nursing homes, schools, and local jails. Drop-off points can be established at a post office, for example, or two-car and three-car garages which may have ample room for temporary storage. And garage sales go on continuously in any community. Instead of trying to bring in a little extra cash for what we own and no longer want, imagine pooling all of that in some temporary space or recycling center so that those in the community with greater need could take what they wanted. Oh, I know some will say that such generosity would be preyed on by those looking to take what they can and then turn around and sell it to make a quick buck. Sure that can happen, but if someone has a need to make a little money one way or another, why should we think of them as predators? What name should we use for those of us who carelessly horde what we no longer need or use?

There is a principle that guides the management of water distribution and allocation in the high desert of northern New Mexico. Water is precious and sometimes very scarce depending on the amount of winter snow melt and other seasonal factors. It is said that the landowners who tend to *acequias*, the irrigation ditches which distribute water among them, "share in the surplus and share in the shortage." I think that is a useful way to think about the pooling of resources in any community, whatever those resources may be—water, food, clothing, all manner of material goods, and time itself. As government now and in the future will find it more difficult to provide resources for those in need, I think the mind-set of what's mine is mine will lose some of its force as we learn to share in the surplus and share in the shortage. "Surplus" is a relative term and there are many different views on what it means at any particular time or place. So, too, with "shortage" or scarcity. I would argue the measure should simply be what resources are available to be pooled and shared in a community. Like a crowd that gathers, what each of us has may seem trivial but when combined with enough others, our pooled resources are likely to be extraordinary.

The Boomer generation not only has the numbers, but those numbers offer resources that can set a new standard of what enough others can do—something of their own making—about a wide range of social problems. The Boomers' own health is bound up in what they can do for themselves and for others beyond the doctor's office. Their abundant education, credentials, and available time are bound up in what they can do for young people beyond the school zone. And their wealth of material possessions and talents can lead on to how they pool and share such resources with those who have far less. This is what may be required of aging Boomers and all of us when government can no longer afford to try and do it for us.

I know that some will think this is dreamy stuff. The social criticism often directed at the Boomers is that they have lost whatever groupieness their protest years gave them—an advantage and public prominence that they no longer seek. Am I then musing about a renewal of collective action that just doesn't fit their generation anymore? If Boomers, given their upbringing and the professional paths they chose, makes them libertarians at heart—"let me do my thing, you do yours"—then is it possible for them to subordinate themselves to some cause or movement that doesn't sufficiently acknowledge each of them or their contributions? It was far easier to subordinate themselves temporarily to the causes and movements of their youth when their standing as free-wheeling adults was still down the road. Now they are far down that road and travel on their own without direction from anybody else, embracing the mantra "you owe it to yourself" and going their own separate ways. As a consequence, for many Boomers, their public lives have shriveled without associational ties and have been reduced to generous impulses, calculations of self-interest, or ideological statements. One central study of the Boomer generation recently done by two observers of the respected Yankelovich firm noted, "The Boomer focus on self is the exaltation of self and the principal spirit of life. Others are not disregarded or dishonored; rather they are simply not that relevant to defining the purpose and focus of life."[47] Their extensive study does not parse, however, the problem that such focus on self presents. What Boomers might still want to accomplish for themselves when it comes to contributing to the resolution of social problems is really not possible unless they do it with others. Anyone and everyone is entitled to garner from self-organizing what each needs in the complex stew of individuality, but it is only possible to meet and satisfy such personal need *with others*. "You do your thing, I'll do mine" is not enough.

What is encouraging, however, about the Boomers' can-do attitude is less reliance on government. Smith and Clurman see them wanting to do it themselves—whatever "it" might become.[48] Certainly the Boomers contributed significantly to social change, usually ahead of or in defiance of government actions, when they engaged in anti-war protests, drug experimentation, sexual freedom, mainstream rock, and the civil rights, environmental, and women's liberation movements. What goes around comes around? Their numbers, always the Boomer numbers remain impressive, and they are approaching a time in their lives when their myriad paths and stories again share a common prospect—what to do with the balance of life which may not be as varied or consuming as the separate paths they have pursued since leaving home. More than thirty years ago, Hannah Pitkin eloquently described what I think might be a central motivation of aging Boomers moving from their intensely private lives to take the lead again in public life: "Surely the right account must be about neither self-interest nor self-sacrifice, but the self-realization of a not yet completed person."[49] Although Pitkin was not writing about any particular generation, "the not yet completed person" could very well describe many Boomers who, as I said at this chapter's beginning, made their peace and found their place in a far from finished culture they had once challenged and helped to move off dead center. If one thinks they now are inseparable from that culture, then they may not see it as unfinished. But Pitkin is talking about the unfinished self and there is good reason to believe that many Boomers may very well see themselves as unfinished and unfulfilled. Once again, self-realization might require a collective experience, a recognition that *only* through their sizable numbers coming together can each of them achieve the self-realization of a "completed person." It is also conceivable that they will form new associations that become affectionate enterprises, not just idealized abstractions to which they become obliged by serving their communities as they find them, not just as they would wish them to be.

Perhaps it will take some precipitating event or events, local, regional, or national, in which aging Boomers find good reason to find each other again and join together. It might be municipal bankruptcy when essential public services become problematic. It might be the largest employer in the area leaving for China and leaving behind unfinished local projects it helped subsidize. It might be a reduction of personnel in hospitals, schools, and recreation facilities that calls for organizing volunteers to fill in where needed. Whether or not such precipitating events will nudge Boomers out of their daily routines is not yet knowable. But their numbers, again their numbers, offer a substantial service force distinct from those consumed by getting to work and raising children and who may not think they have the time. Aging Boomers may very well have the gift of time that others cannot afford or find elusive. Of course, many Boomers, for one reason or another, will not willingly abandon the careers and other pursuits they have become accustomed to in their middle years. They may say, "Look, I can't afford to turn my attention to self-organizing and new social practices. I am still in a rat race that I can't leave." Time, however, works in many different ways and what may once have seemed an indulgence in finding time for a long-neglected passion may take on a fresh urgency when looking over the actuarial tables. The very reason that I'm writing this book is, in part, driven by a fresh urgency to organize and share a point of view that has been long in development and now seems to me to be especially timely when so many have given up on government or perhaps have given up on themselves.

Theodore Roszak, that once unintended spokesperson for the Boomer generation, before his death took up the Boomer generation story again and with his gift of optimism predicted that, "What Boomers left undone in their youth, they will return to take up in their maturity, if for no other reason than because they will want to make old age interesting." Roszak saw such renewal leading to "the creation of new social forms and cultural possibilities."[50] Roszak saw what Pitkin does—the opportunity for "self-realization of a not yet completed person." The very peace that Boomers made with the established order leaves many of them with unfinished business and Roszak saw that too. Roszak predicted "a spreading network of mutual aid" driven by "the simple and inevitable process of aging."[51] That certainly may be true when it comes to the social problem of health care, their own and others. And from there, I take the self-realization argument further to include helping to educate the young beyond the school zone and pooling resources for those who otherwise may go without. Roszak believed the discontent of the Boomers in the 1960s was "healthy, even if it lacked the competence to survive."[52] Surely, now with so many intervening years and with so many using their professional credentials, Boomers will bring greater experience and competence to those undertakings they find attractive or necessary. They are not likely to coalesce, however, into one or more national undertakings, nor will the self-organizing and new social practices they may pursue recreate the protest conditions and social movements of the 1960s and 1970s. There are likely to be many different pathways they create and follow with some becoming major avenues that take all of us further and faster. Again, I come back to the Boomer numbers. As one of them has said: "The truth is, we are important because there are so many of us."[53] The numbers are impressive when by 2030 the elderly population will have doubled. By then all of the Boomers will have crossed the 65-year-old threshold—70 to 80 million Boomers aged 65 to 84. How can anyone ignore what they might do—something of their own making. Their numbers, always their numbers.

CHAPTER 5

One Thing Can Lead to Another

Some think that if we shrink the size of government somehow everything will turn out OK. Nope, I'm sorry: the aging Boomers—their numbers alone—won't shrink health care costs just because public treasuries are squeezed; whatever the budget is for public education, our schools are still not producing the kind of educated citizens we need; and those in poverty will become even more vulnerable if shrunken government cannot provide an adequate safety net. Consequently, this concluding chapter assumes that our social attention and self-organizing could very well move front and center, gaining the attention of public office holders, the professional establishment, and online news sites as one thing leads to another.

Working with Government's Support

I can imagine a newly elected officeholder shaping her remarks in new ways for us at an open meeting: "Good evening. It is customary to ask for your support when undertaking the public agenda my colleagues and I now confront. The times we now live in, however, are different. So I come to you not asking for your support but asking how I can use my public office to support you. Yes, you heard it right. I want to do all

---

A portion of a section of this chapter, "Deliberating with the Professionals," is previous work of mine, "Public Grieving and Public Thinking," *Higher Education Exchange* (2002): 6–12, and has been reprinted and adapted with the permission of the Kettering Foundation.

I can to support your efforts to address social problems which are beyond the means of government without your social attention and self-organizing. I'm talking about what you are doing to provide health care beyond the doctor's office, education beyond the school zone, and to pool your resources for those less fortunate."

With that she waves a copy of *The Real Change-Makers*. After failing to launch a standing ovation, I sit down and the officeholder goes on. "Yes, I think the book is a wake-up call for all of us—a new way to think about our social problems. As you know, those of us in government have little money in the public till to support your efforts but we do have assets that can be put at your disposal. Let me share some of them with you now and in the days and months to come: We have an abundance of public buildings that we can keep open for those occasions when you want to meet with us or just among yourselves; we have a multitude of websites that can feature what you are doing; we can establish recognition awards for those of you who have won the special respect and affection of others; and we have the capacity to use what statistical measures seem appropriate to quantify what you are doing for yourselves and others. I'm sure the numbers are impressive and we can use them for your sake and our government's sake too."

I can imagine, at this point, the public officeholder pausing for a moment before going on with a broad smile as she introduces the subject of perks. "Now, many of you may not know much about the perks of public office, and rightly so since many officeholders would rather you not know about *their* perks. That's perks for *perquisites,* which Webster's Dictionary defines as "privileges, gains, or profits incidental to regular salary or wages." For those in government office, perks may include free passes at toll booths or racetracks, parking permits, and, for the newly elected, a dressing up of whatever office they occupy. They will tell you, after all, that they promised to clean house, which obviously means decorating it too, with new draperies and a carpet so thick your shoes don't show. And last, but not the least, is an automobile that comes with at least a reading lamp and, of course, an assigned driver. After all, it is impossible to use a reading lamp in the back seat if you have to drive the car yourself. But let's get serious. Government can't afford perks anymore. At least, I don't think it should, and whatever is still budgeted for perks I want to put at your disposal—my office for meetings to keep track of what we're both doing, my parking permits, my toll passes, and my driver if he can help some of you get around."

The officeholder then concludes her remarks. "I was born nearby where we are meeting, and I have always tried to look after things as I find them. Some of you are locals like me. Some of you come from somewhere else and you want to change what you've found here. I think all of us have work to do, and the time has come, in fact it is long overdue, for public officials like me and citizens like you to come together, not just to share this one evening, but on a regular basis to deliberate about what other social problems need attention, what social practices we already have that could be adopted for this or that problem, and what new social practices could help. I want to support such deliberation in any way I can, which means bringing my professional staff, consulting experts, and pollsters together with you to explore such questions and any others you might want to share. If this sounds out of tune with what you have assumed top-down government is like, then it's obvious I have a lot of work to do, along with my political and professional colleagues, to turn over a new leaf. I happen to believe that there are many, many more of us on both sides of the government/citizen divide ready to change the ways things get done. You have already pursued many new and different paths for solving social problems, and you deserve a different attitude from those of us in government about who are the real change-makers. If you still think it's not you and enough others like you, I can assure you it ain't me or anyone else in government."

Of course, I wrote the speech for the public officeholder, which was easy. Getting an official to deliver it in the real world might take a little more time and effort, but one thing can lead to another, and the point of her imagined remarks is that there are all kinds of possibilities once the momentum shifts to the citizen side of the street. Government support for emerging social practices should get more attention as governments at every level find it more difficult to spend the money and deliver the services that in better times most people took for granted.

When I cited John Stuart Mill in the first chapter who said that government is wrong when it tolerates "no experiments but its own," it underscores that government's work involves experiments just as our own social practices do. As we learn from trial and error when seeking social change, so, too, does government learn, and there should be many more crossovers between us when it comes to the zigzag paths of social problem solving.[1] Such government attention to what citizens are doing should not arise just because of a pending election or because there are dwindling funds in government accounts. It should be an acknowledgment that local knowledge about social problems and how to deal with them is situated in those communities who have experienced the problems, not just studied them though various professional lenses some distance from the local scene.[2] Our bottom-up social attention and self-organizing should therefore lead, not follow, what government may choose to do about social problems in the future. We may start off on many different paths, some leading to the other side of the forest, others ending in thickets too dense to penetrate. But whatever paths prove reliable, it would help to have the support of government performing an integrative function of putting more citizens in touch with those who succeed in getting through the forest.

Without great cost in dollars and cents, we know that many *government mandates* have proved their worth. Some libertarians still object to wearing seat belts in cars or helmets when riding motorcycles, putting aside their cell phones when driving, not smoking in public places, or picking up after their dogs on city sidewalks. In New Hampshire where we lived, a state that still wrestles with its libertarian heritage, seat belts are only required for children, not adults. The state's motto remains, "Live Free or Die." For adults without seat belts, I think their motto might just as well be, "live free *and* die." Furthermore, we forget that many government mandates have been our doing when certain social practices have become law through our urging. After all, it's easier to tell a careless dog walker to pick up after his pet because "it's the law," than to lecture him on sidewalk cleanliness. The expectation is that most of us will comply, however, not because of the threat of enforcement, but because enough of our fellow citizens insisted that we change some of our habits. When our behavior encounters social disapproval, new practices are certainly reinforced with government mandates, but more than likely we find ourselves doing what others are doing by going along to get along.

It is also useful to consider what government might do to encourage new social practices, whose scope and reach might be greatly enhanced by what Cass Sunstein and Richard Thaler think of as government nudges. Sunstein, before going to the Obama White House as head of the Office of Information and Regulatory Affairs, co-wrote an important book with Thaler titled *Nudge*. The book explores what government can do to help us do what is socially constructive without requiring us to do it. Nudges, not mandates, is their focus. Nudges are as simple as dealing with the roadside litter problem in Texas when that state government posted signs, "Don't Mess With Texas." Within the first six years there was a 72 percent reduction in roadside litter.[3] The advantage of nudges is that those who don't need to be nudged are exempt. Nudges are only for those who need them. Mandates don't work that way. Their book is full of nudge examples that make government more the sly motivator than the heavy-handed rule maker so many find intrusive. We are certainly accustomed to the nudging of the marketplace where for-profits relentlessly try to push our buying habits this way or that or the selective incentives of not-for-profits, which offer tote bags for contributing $50 or more, a 5 percent discount on car rentals, or group tours for joining an alumni association. And Sunstein and Thaler think that anyone can be a nudge, or what they more elegantly describe as a "choice architect," who organizes "the context in which people make decisions." Their examples include doctors who propose alternative treatments, parents presenting education options for their children, and those who design ballots for elections. They conclude that "[t]o count as a mere nudge, the intervention must be easy and cheap to avoid."[4]

So beyond what my imagined, newly elected officeholder offered in support, what mandates and nudges could government assemble to support our social attention to providing health care beyond the doctor's office, educating young people beyond the school zone, and pooling our resources for those in need? Certainly, government support for such social practices can mean more than just being a cheerleader on the sidelines. For example, when others' bad habits impose certain health costs on all of us, such habits can be taxed, which already accounts for various government efforts to impose a tax on sugary sodas that contribute to obesity. With governments in difficult fiscal straits it makes sense to put a few cents more on soda purchases, not only to discourage consumption, but to use the tax revenues to pay for the added health costs arising from such consumption. It is estimated that the average American drinks about a gallon of sweetened beverages a week.[5] Government went so far in its anti-smoking campaign as to ban cigarette advertising. The same advertising ban could be considered for products that seduce the tastes of those whose obesity we all have to pay for. The provocative question that libertarians raise is "to what extent should we use the power of the state to protect us from ourselves?"[6] Gregory Mankiw's question, however, raises an interesting counter question about his assumption that my well-being is mainly my business only. Doesn't my ill health affect those I live with and add to the health costs that others may bear? Such interdependence is unavoidable, and what the libertarian question misses is that, like it or not, my health or ill health is other people's business. When we spend $150 billion a year treating obesity-related conditions, those are everyone's dollars.[7]

Just think of the many ways that government can make health care more affordable or free up more funds to pay for it. Consider the effects of reducing federal subsidies that support agribusiness and its alignment with those products that contribute to the growing problem of obesity, and consider how federal subsidies instead could help support local greenmarkets with their more nutritious offerings. Consider what targeted tuition subsidies could do to get more medical students choosing to become primary care doctors rather than specialists. Consider what a serious review of accreditation and licensing requirements could do to improve custodial services for those who need them, with some allowance for volunteers to be more integral in the delivery of such services.[8] Consider lifting the restraints on buying cheaper prescription drugs from Canada and abroad to drive down the costs of what the pharmaceutical industry can charge for brand name drugs in the United States. Consider requiring restaurants to include the calorie intake for items on their menus.[9] Finally, consider legislative action superseding judicial precedents that would give doctors' patients the option to waive the right to sue, thus removing some of the costs of defensive medicine that doctors practice to protect themselves from malpractice litigation.[10] As a once practicing lawyer, I am quite aware of the self-interest involved in pursuing expensive litigation on behalf of clients. The United States has more lawyers per capita than any country in the world, and the fierce competition to earn a comfortable professional living means that the interests of clients and their attorneys are almost indistinguishable when they agree as follows: If the client fails to recover, she owes the lawyer nothing, but if the client succeeds, the lawyer gets a hefty part of whatever amount is recovered. Such contingency fee arrangements certainly have no value for anyone else including the medical establishment and the health care costs borne by the rest of us.

When it comes to encouraging exercise that underlies better health in so many ways, local governments have many options wherever there are open public spaces not utilized. There should be no limit to the imagination of citizens and government officials to make such space more attractive to those who want or need to exercise.[11] Recognition awards to those already engaged in promoting healthy lifestyles in a community is always a government option, and whenever there are bureaucratic hangups and logjams for those wanting to use public spaces, they should be cleared away. Insurance companies, alone or in cooperation with government agencies, can also provide incentives such as health club and gym membership discounts. And what about tax breaks for employers with onsite fitness facilities? These are just a few of the options that governments either are pursuing or could pursue.[12]

When it comes to education beyond the school zone, the obvious place to start is how community educators can better connect with public schools, which are under local and state jurisdiction and which have a host of financial and policy ties with the federal government as well. Rather than ignoring those who provide their own civic curricula in after-school hours or on weekends, school administrators and teachers looking for allies can learn from such community educators and could integrate what is being done beyond the school zone in their classrooms and extra-curricular activities they offer.[13] There is also the potential of democratic circles, which I discussed in chapter 4, which often get short shrift in the classroom but is a practice that could vastly improve what little civic education is now pursued during school hours. As for mentors, learn what they're doing and bring them into the classroom so more young people can have the benefit of their experience or personal expertise. Those citizens who have reached out to school dropouts could also be welcomed and serve as bridges back for those young people wanting to return. Since government usually hands out money based on how many students are enrolled, the work of community educators and mentors to recover dead-end young lives and put them back on track is currently undervalued.

When enough others pool their resources for those in need, their example should obviously be honored and broadcast by governments whose own means are increasingly limited.[14] We know that government itself is a form of pooling resources. It takes our money in the form of tax dollars and spends it where it thinks we want our dollars to go—sometimes. Such spending programs certainly will not disappear just because we scale up the social practice of pooling our resources. Our tax dollars will not be refunded anytime soon, but with the enormous political pressures to curtail taxing and spending, our resource pooling efforts are likely to be more valued. There again, government has many ways to encourage and support our resource pooling so that those in need can share in our surplus rather than just share in the government's shortage.

Deliberating with the Professionals

Across the country, the unprecedented events of September 11, 2001, prompted what I would call public grieving. In New York City in particular, public places were crowded with strangers looking for each other, looking out for each other, sharing their shock, their grief, and their mutual vulnerability. There were spontaneous gatherings on street corners and in parks, in front of fire stations and hospitals, wherever New Yorkers were drawn to in the wake of such horror. It was an extraordinary time in which the anonymity so prized in big city life became a difficult burden for many people. In familiar places, unfamiliar faces gave and received comfort. Public grieving was palpable everywhere.[15]

I was drawn to the park in Union Square, not far from where I worked and taught and only two miles from ground zero in lower Manhattan. Union Square is a place with a colorful history, once a site for mansions and artists, theatre and nightlife, labor protests and derelicts. For a time even the politically notorious Tammany Hall held sway there. More recently, the Square hosts a prominent greenmarket where farmers and artisans sell their produce and wares from the backs of pickup trucks and vans. The park in the center of the Square is a familiar place where rollerbladers meet up, street entertainers and religious zealots vie for attention, and dog owners, teeny boppers, and the curious congregate.

As I related in chapter 3, what I saw both day and night that September in the Square and its park were strangers expressing an urgent need to communicate their feelings and thoughts in a public space with public witnesses. It occurred to me then that public thinking is like public grieving. They are both, to paraphrase Michael Sandel, what we can only know in common and do together. They arise from a narrative ground in which all of us are necessarily joined as neighbors, community members, and citizens when confronted by events and their implications that need to be shared. The scene at Union Square, however, was not a coherent public assembly. There was no convening group or agenda or deliberative process. People moved in and out, as I did from day to day, treating it like a greenmarket of fresh feeling and thought but without an outcome that anyone could know or report. There was public thinking here and there and from time to time, but it was not so much intentional as it was a by-product of the shock and grieving that brought people there in the first place.

At the time, I wondered if there would be opportunities in the days and weeks ahead for public thinking arising out of the events of that September 11. Who would be convener and what would be the agenda and process used? I thought perhaps my university and its new president would take the lead. Within a day after the attack the university had been willing to open its doors to those seeking some word about their loved ones from a neighboring hospital. The university had provided hospitality and counseling for survivors looking for survivors. Ad hoc forums of faculty and students also emerged for what one facilitator called a "genuine conversation," and, for a time, many classrooms became places for storytelling and probing about what had happened.

As weeks passed, I found that public grieving in the university neighborhood evolved mainly into tender and impressive forms of public thanking and public giving. Just below Union Square in the 14th Street subway station and adjacent to a police squad office where two of its members were missing, I saw tangible expressions of thanks and condolences from schoolchildren from Long Island to Texas. Their heartfelt messages extended down a white-tiled passageway for several hundred feet where, for example, the second grade class of Mrs. Riegal and Ms. Tree affixed their poster: "Dear Rescuers, You are our Heroes." It was just one of the many public spaces across the city where public thanking was on display to honor fire, police, and emergency personnel and in remembrance of their fallen colleagues. The public giving was everywhere in an outpouring of contributions, both spontaneous and carefully organized. A news account written near ground zero described an evangelical group from Louisville moving among small business owners and writing checks from $1,000 to $3,000 on the spot as a simple gesture of immediate help—no applications, no strings attached. By contrast, the same account quoted a spokesman for a more established charity who said that its response was "based on professional social work . . . we're not trying to do something outside our expertise."[16]

The same professionalism could describe my university's response as it settled down to offering its resident expertise to civic coalitions, nonprofit agencies, and private employers. The most prominent effort was consumed with what should become of the devastated Trade Center site. At a vast intersection of public and private interests, rebuilding lower Manhattan was seen as the most visible, if not the most pressing, challenge confronting the city. At the outset, it seemed that most of the pro bono experts took for granted that public officials legitimately represented the public in such matters, and those citizens most affected were seen as victims, not partners. Nonetheless, parents in schools near ground zero, a downtown coalition of residents, and those who lost loved ones on September 11 insisted that they have some say in the redevelopment. At the time, I wondered aloud to a colleague whether there would be an opportunity in the days and weeks ahead for public deliberation arising out of the events of September 11. I recalled in chapter 2 his response: "Oh, wouldn't that be ideal but you know as well as I do,

David, that's not the way the system works." He just assumed that professional contributions were the most competent means available to whatever given end they served.

My colleague ignored, however, an inconvenient fact that professional thinking often overlooks. Public ends are rarely given, they must be constructed, and that is neither the job nor within the special competencies of specialists, academic or otherwise. Public thinking and professional thinking are not the same. At its core, public thinking is centered on ends, on the important questions of "Where are we going?" "Is this desirable?" "What should be done?"[17] Such questions are just that—questions. They have to be shared before they can be answered. When you and I ask genuine questions, not rhetorical ones, we are looking for help. We are looking for others who can enlarge our understanding. The supposed shortcut that professionals take of looking at the data of individual opinion aggregated in poll surveys misses the point. Without questions to share, we only have our preconceived opinions and answers, meager resources when confronted with problems beyond any one person's resolution. Public thinking, like public grieving, is not something that anyone can do alone.

Professional thinking does not operate in a vacuum either, but its forums often disappoint. That December, just up the street from Union Square but a world away from the spontaneous and disordered ceremonies of public grieving, my university hosted a conference on "New York City at a Turning Point." In the lobby outside the auditorium, those on the invite list deposited their business cards in a glass bowl. They represented an array of urban organizations—academic, financial, philanthropic, civic, governmental. This weekday-morning conference was another occasion for these professionals to listen to their peers and network during coffee breaks. The university's president welcomed them, noting the significance of 10 universities located near ground zero and the likelihood that those attending could come up with "solutions" given the "intellect and passions" in the hall. I couldn't tell if he was flattering them or whether he really believed that this university-hosted conference would provide some kind of policy breakthrough.

One of the academic presenters, a political scientist, spoke eloquently of a "civic conversation" underway, but it turned out to be the high stakes lobbying she thought was needed in Washington, DC, in conjunction with "mobilizing public opinion and educating them."

Another presenter, an economist from the Citizens Budget Commission, recommended that the cost of the safety net to help low-income residents should be shifted from the city to the state because "it is the right thing to do." When I asked her during a coffee break whether her viewpoint reflected citizen input, she reminded me that the commission had no such link except through its trustees.

The keynote speaker was an elected public official and candidate for governor who called for using a moribund financial control board composed of the governor, mayor, state and city comptrollers, and three private sector representatives as an open forum for dealing with the serious fiscal problems confronting New York City. His speech was laced with references to community, the business community, the labor community, a "new community" in lower Manhattan, but, except for the families of victims, he thought the question of what should be done with the Trade Center site belonged to those responsible for the financing. Like all the presenters, he acknowledged public needs without seeing a reason for public thinking about what those needs were or should be. Instead he thanked the presenters for their data and forecasts and then moved to the lobby to take questions from the media. As I sat there listening to one presenter after another probe the economic and psychological consequences of September 11, I realized that they were as much at a loss as those I had been with in Union Square. But unlike the impromptu forums in the park, the conference presentations offered only the standard monologue with a perfunctory Q and A to follow. The conference-goers were there to learn but had little chance to participate. I thought to myself, *If New York City is "at a turning point," how can there be a productive exchange about the choices to be made in a darkened auditorium of note scribblers and PowerPoint presentations?* It was like a bad classroom.

The format and work product of the conference was such a predictable standard for the discussion of public issues that no one thought to ask, "But where is the public?" When I turned to express my concern about the absence of public thinking to a conference-goer from the city comptroller's office, she tried to reassure me that there was indeed a lot going on elsewhere, "multiple channels" as she called them, at school-parent associations and community boards. She could not reassure me, however, that such channels intersected with the professional thinking on display in the auditorium or with private sector stakeholders and public officials. When I raised the same concern with another conference-goer, he shrugged, "Oh, that's the stuff of public hearings, don't you think?"

How wrong he was. Public hearings are definitely not where public thinking gets done. Testimony is taken, a record is made, but very little else is developed. Advocates, with their minds already made up, come to make a statement and, like the conference of professionals, listen to others make their statements. Neither venue leaves anything to chance or to the development of a conversation in which participants engage each other. The New York State Assembly held a public hearing soon after my university's forum, and in the notice of public hearing, the chairs of four legislative committees announced that a "collective vision for the future of New York City can be developed only by listening to and learning from governmental agencies, public authorities, utility providers, other businesses and community groups impacted by the events of September 11th." They went on to stipulate that oral testimony would be limited to fifteen minutes' duration. It was the public's turn with no time for public thinking.

After the conference, I headed back to Union Square. Part of it had become a parking lot for construction vehicles as the park was renovated. Another part was occupied temporarily by the red-and-white-striped tents of tradesman selling their holiday wares. The public grieving and public thanking and public giving had moved to other venues. But where were the venues for public thinking about the "what should be" questions? Where were the intersections for professionals and citizens still bewildered by what had happened to sit down as equals and sort out what they could learn from each other and what they should do—together?

I returned to those questions in writing this book after posing them in my work ten years ago. Back then, I gained some satisfaction when a few months after September 11, I attended "Listening to the City," an event serving as the kick-off of a six-month process of civic conversations that included a mix of professional and citizen focus groups. It became a new but temporary venue for public thinking that intersected with the self-described "community of professionals" working the system as best they could to rebuild downtown New York. I must say, however, that the very slow redevelopment of Ground Zero and the surrounding neighborhood didn't show much of the effects of those civic conversations. Still, some professionals in the system did try to cross over and meet with citizens, those directly affected by September 11 and those eager to take part, for whatever such conversations might produce.

I can imagine that, if our social attention and self-organizing scaled up enough to impress at least some of today's professionals in their policy warrens of credentialed expertise, one thing could lead to another. Just listen to one such voice at the imagined open meeting I began the chapter with. A professional consultant, taking a cue from the newly elected government official we already heard from, joins us, so to speak, at the open meeting.

"I look forward to sitting down with you all in whatever deliberative forum we can construct together. My client in top-down government thinks that the time has come for all of us to 'deliberate as equals.' I agree with her. I know that public ends are rarely given. They must be constructed and that process is not something to be delegated to people like me and my policy-wonk colleagues. And I think we should also include representatives from NGOs, who I know try to serve your interests but often neglect to include you in their deliberations. From my experience they are more often collaborators with those of us in government than with those of you who may be their members. Yes, I know we all seek your input from time to time, but I'm afraid real consultation is usually limited to our closed professional circles. I have no idea what can emerge from our deliberations, but if it is anything like my peer conversations with other professionals, it will be neither predictable nor merely the sum of individual contributions. If you agree, let's also invite pollsters to join us. They regularly report about your preferences and opinions, but aggregate such one-on-one inquiries rather than letting something develop out of a shared conversation. Instead of their posing the questions, let our deliberation together frame the questions that form the basis of what we then share in an ongoing conversation. We might also consider using online resources to construct a conversation extending to those who may not be able to join us here given their work schedules, health, or family obligations. It is relatively costless online and we are likely to reach a much wider range of thinking and experience. However constructed, we should think of our deliberations as a work in progress."

With that the professional consultant nods to his newly elected client and takes his leave. My imagining his offer of deliberation is within the realm of possibility *if* our social attention and social practices take hold with one thing leading to another. My argument throughout has been that the culture of professionalism can change if we are seen again as the real change-makers. Why? It has been my experience that I know far less than what other people think I do. This impression has led me to believe that many professionals may know far less than we think they do—that our culture of professionalism rests on a kind of unstated pretension. Deliberation does not so much challenge that pretension as it lets everyone share what they can add, thus enriching the conversation far beyond what is possible when too much deference is paid to the few with credentials.[18] We are all control freaks, at one time or another, but it is especially common among professionals who want to shape public issues to fit their expertise. When there are no opportunities for deliberation, all they have are their respective hammers and "everything looks like a nail." That can't happen when framing a social problem becomes a joint venture with citizens. The hammer metaphor gets at the heart of why experts are far from being adequate substitutes when it comes to dealing with complicated social problems and why deliberating should be far more than the polite solicitation of community input. Deliberating as equals with experts makes it more than just a gripe session or bull session. What can emerge from such conversations is the discovery on everyone's part that they have a great deal to learn from each other. The "I don't know enough" excuse is just that when new social practices belie what we once thought was only our marginal role in dealing with social problems. I like James C. Scott's wonderful analogy of sea captains and harbormasters. The professional sea captains bring their large vessels into our local waters but as harbormasters we are needed to bring their ships to safe docking. Their professional knowledge of the broad seas and our local knowledge of complicated inlets are both needed.[19] It's not easy bringing an ocean liner manned by professionals to dock without the help of those on the local scene who have experienced, not just studied, social problems. The answers are found in the doing not just the examination of the problems. What experts bring to the conversation is the proprietary knowledge of their respective fields. What citizens bring is the public knowledge they have acquired by working through a social problem with self-organizing and the social practices they have developed together. Both kinds of knowledge are important.

For those professionals who remain immodest despite their limitations when deliberating with us, we should consider asking what I have called a "stupid" but important question: "Just how does your expertise relate to the social problems we are wrestling with?" Then it might be the expert's turn to ask us: "What is it that you know that I need to know?" As the newly elected officeholder noted, such an exchange would start us off on an equal footing for deliberating on some broad questions: What social problems need attention? What social practices do we already have that could be adopted for this or that problem? What new social practices could help? Asking such questions and others, developed and shared, requires the exercise of public judgment. Such judgment is certainly not reserved to experts. Public judgment exercised in a deliberative forum is more a collective understanding of what is possible to do about a problem. That is why pollsters would have much to learn when deliberating with us too. Public judgment arises from deliberation; public opinion is little more than individual opinions statistically aggregated.[20] Like professionals on NGO staffs, pollsters also make a map of a social problem in their heads and then test the adequacy of such a map by asking what we think. When deliberating, however, with us as equals, any map would be the co-creation of experts, pollsters, and the rest of us.[21] Otherwise, experts often define the questions for us if they dominate the public conversation. They end up determining what our needs are rather than deliberating with us about what we think our needs are. This is the point of view of John McKnight, an intellectual pioneer in seeing how the culture of professionalism has misshaped and retarded the potential of community members looking after themselves.[22]

In deliberating together, professionals may discover that it is not enough to see a social problem objectively, that it is also important to learn how a particular problem appears subjectively to citizens who have actually experienced the problem—what I cited earlier as "social learning." Our social learning is invaluable in getting us engaged in new social practices, and sharing that learning with professionals can enlarge their understanding of what they might contribute in helping us.[23] I wrote earlier in chapter 2 about "the politics of social problem solving"—deliberating with an expert is also a form of such politics. If we deliberate as equals within a democratic circle, it's not enough for the expert to think he knows what the problem is. It also matters what *we* think the problem is. It is not enough for the expert to think he knows what the solution is. It also matters whether *we* think his solution fits our own conception of what the problem is. And even if his solution does, it is possible that we may think that we have better solutions than his.

In any deliberation among equals, it is not just a matter of bringing experts and pollsters into the circle but also acknowledging the differences among citizens already in the circle. They do not come as one voice, but many voices reflecting different experiences, different opinions, and different expectations. If ideas for yet more social practices emerge, are they congenial to everyone's everyday lives? Will some find it difficult to participate? Have they had the opportunity to have their say? Does the new social practice make sense in one place but not another? Doubling back to be sure everyone has been heard is important or otherwise the outcomes of a deliberation can become the property of some but not others—just as government solutions or placebos become the property of well-meaning professionals who leave too much out and too many of us as well. No one in the room can think for us—that's what deliberation is all about.[24] My colleague at the Kettering Foundation, David Mathews, put it well: "We do not have to agree but we do have to share."[25]

Making the News

After hearing from the newly elected office holder offering various forms of support and the hired professional gun seeking to deliberate with us as equals, the voice of someone who is covering the event is heard from the back. She stands up to be heard.

"What is 'news' is a choice that the 24/7 media makes everyday, and local news has been a serious casualty in the overall financial decline of print journalism from which the other media feed.[26] It's time for those of us who are tired of local news consisting mainly of weather, crime, and accident coverage to do something more. Too much is going on under the media radar that needs coverage and amplification. Your social attention and social practices deserve more of our attention. You should know that there are many news gatherers like me who want to spread the word of what you're doing and track your progress from bottom-up efforts to the tipping point of regional and national change. We think that's a story worth covering. I represent a point of view that the 24/7 mainstream media should not be the only force 'making the news.' If we help to facilitate what you've done, I think there will be many more newly elected and incumbent office holders, along with the experts and pollsters who circle those nests, who will want to get on the right side of history where you have already staked your claim. So how do we get them there?

"There are more and more news sites online, like mine, that are feeding the mainstream press who, like government, are going through serious fiscal retrenchment. Our news sites are also feeding the appetites of local TV stations and all-news cable channels. 'Outsourcing' the news is becoming increasingly common and since many emerging news sites have modest bottom-up origins, I think that we have much in common. Your social attention and our social attention can be joined. So, with all of you as abundant sources, together we can 'make the news.' Our websites can also facilitate online deliberation if those interested are unable to join you in 'live' deliberations. And there's no reason why we can't wean some pundits from their blog sites and put them on equal footing with you on our news sites. I know that there are some who think that those online don't show the same mutual respect for each other that

they do when face-to-face, but it's worth trying.[27] Establishing deliberative domains online can be a very different asynchronous process, but,
if classroom courses can be productive online, I don't know why our
tinkering with the process of citizen deliberation can't succeed as well.
You'll be the judge anyway, not just folks like me. We already know
that the Wikipedia model is pretty successful as an example of an open
source technique where 'the intelligence' garnered is 'simply emergent.'[28]
I'm sure that some of your coworkers, friends and neighbors will click
on regularly to follow and perhaps join what you have already so successfully undertaken. There will always be new social practices to track
and new ways of doing old things, both of which will have a better
chance of taking hold if online news sites tell the stories and stay with
them as they succeed, fail, change their spots—whatever. So I hope you'll
find digital newsgathering as a productive way to tell your stories. It
could be our biggest story for a long time to come."

With that our new friend and ally, the news gatherer, takes a deep
breath and sits down.

It's unlikely that we will see a reversal of the now dominant form of
news organization ownership that has moved from local owners to dis-
tant corporate interests content with more and more junk news. As Alex
Jones puts it, "We seem poised to be a nation overfed but undernour-
ished." A kind of couch potato citizen obesity or, as Jones describes, "a
culture of people waddling around, swollen with media exposure."[29]
Citizen journalism, however, could offer a healthy diet that can do all
of us some good—obese or not. First came the proponents of "public
journalism" in the 1990s, whose newspapers challenged the detached
neutrality of mainstream journalism. Then, public journalism moved on
to "civic journalism" as online weblogs put more news gathering and
opinion making in the hands of a varied lot of citizen-observers. One
commentator saw this shift as public journalism "morphing into the
public's journalism."[30] What remains is a point of view that journalism
is a public practice, a social practice at that, which should put politics
and public affairs once again within the reach of citizens.[31] Much of
what our friend from the rear of the hall told us about new news sources
is the public's journalism, and it is gaining traction. What used to be
only in the editorial pages of newspapers now is found on websites with
their own editorials, citizen comments, summaries of public forums, and
investigative reporting. Who knows, maybe even the mainstream media
may learn something and make their own adjustments to accommodate
what *we* are doing, not what *they* think is newsworthy elsewhere.

And those Texas billboards I cited before should remind us that government itself has numerous ways of reaching the public through websites, public notices in newspapers, and, of course, the ever-attentive media. As a source of news, when government speaks, the 24/7 media listens and so do we. Government can usually *make* the news on whatever front it chooses, and all of this potential can also be used to advance citizens' efforts who may find it much harder to get public attention.[32] If government spokespersons were to spend more time telling the public what other citizens are doing, it would be a valuable public service for those looking to add to their numbers for whatever new social practices have taken hold but are in need of more amplification. Let couch potato citizens discover how many of their fellow citizens are already involved. Numbers can be very persuasive, so rooted in plain fact.

Like a town crier, news outlets, online or otherwise, and government websites are valuable sources for getting the word out about what core groups are doing in helping to scale up new social practices. As I've said over and over again, so much depends on getting enough others to join in who have been less sure of what needs to be done or whether they wanted to do it. To the extent that so many of them are absorbed in listening to the news, watching the news, or reading the news every day, when they discover their community or neighborhood is actually making the news, who knows? No longer couch potato citizens, no longer pointing the finger at government, instead finding plenty to do and finding each other to do it together. Such folks become part of making the news. They no longer just consume it.[33]

Where Is Your Social Attention?

It's your turn now to take this book's argument in directions that you care most about. Where is your social attention and what social practices would you like to see emerge and scale up? It starts with you and, of course, enough others who share your focus and enthusiasm. I have already looked at three social problems, which I think are of critical concern, related to health, education and social welfare, but one thing can lead to another. There are many, many other social problems within our reach. Social conditions become social problems when you and enough others say they are. That's why I have tried to recount our self-organizing history, to analyze what it takes to get enough others to join in, and to entertain the prospect of aging Boomers playing an important part wherever a critical mass of citizens gets to work.

The origins of new social practices have much in common with established social practices that we are already familiar with. "New" is a relative term, much as we say "nothing new under the sun." So let me mention a few old practices that have practical application for the social problems that you may want to do something about. Persuading others to join you may be easier when they can see that the tried and true is bound up in what you do and what you hope they will do. For example, establishing a new recycling center for sharing the surplus of your community has many obvious precedents of common sense practices that organize others' *uncertainties* of where to go or when to go—lost and founds, bulletin boards, bus stops, annual meetings as examples. The practice of pooling resources itself is also nothing new. Think of pot-luck dinners, libraries, blood banks, museums, credit unions, and ones that I have already noted like food pantries, community gardens, and thrift shops. *Deputizing* others to help with specific tasks has a distinguished lineage. Think of search parties, volunteer firemen, citizen patrols, adopt-a-highway crews, or the simple practice of asking a stranger to keep an eye on your luggage at the airport while you go to the washroom. And any new social practice may be reinforced by reminding others what we already do together to meet particular community needs such as jury duty or blood drives and using litter barrels or collection plates. With the social attention and social practices of enough others, we can put old means to new ends—a kind of social recycling.

I should point out that unintended consequences can also arise when one thing leads to another. Yes, we can self-organize but we also should be alert to what can happen along the way. First, the positive: new social practices may help with other social problems that were not our original focus. Who knows what good things might come when families once again share home-cooked meals and conversation around the dinner table instead of sitting around a TV munching in silence? Who knows what good things might come when parents pay more attention to what their children eat at school, and thus develop an increasing interest in what else schools are doing or not doing for their children? Who knows what good things might come when more of us use the second opinion of reliable websites for health care guidance and become less dependent on professional attention and more attentive to what we can share with friends and coworkers? If community educators and mentors help more young people develop their own capacities for community problem solving, perhaps those young future citizens will undertake more projects of their own that contribute to the general welfare. If more of us discover that we can get along without so much stuff in attics and garages, maybe we'll find the time and money to do even more for those who need help. Like a stone thrown into a pool of water, new social practices and old ones renewed can send ripples in all directions beyond our immediate aim.[34] The fertility of new social practices can spread from one context to another and nothing would be more productive and exciting than to see how others use their imaginations and combine their efforts to extend what you and others have done perhaps far removed from where you started.

On the other hand, the success of a social practice may unintentionally have some negative consequences, something I mentioned in closing chapter 3. There is no fixed storyline for any undertaking. Government may be welcomed in supporting our self-organizing and the outcomes it produces, but some in government may then act in a heavy-handed fashion and assume that they can somehow replace our energies with their own. In this day and age, that's less likely to happen with governments hamstrung with limited resources, but you never know with some in your crowd finding it easier to withdraw and ask government to somehow take the lead. NGOs may also see a good thing and seek to appropriate what you and others have done. Now, neither government nor NGOs will necessarily screw up what you have done without them, but it's a caution anyway that I offer here.

When you and others get around to telling the story of what happened, you will no doubt tidy up some of the loose ends, but the story will surely have many other chapters not of your doing. After all, one thing can lead to another when working with government's support, deliberating with the professionals, and making the news, online or elsewhere. Let governments find in their vast portfolios inexpensive ways to help secure new social practices of our own making. Let the culture of professionalism begin to change so that what we think of as *their* problem-solving preserves become open-source avenues where all of us can travel together. Let the making of news be more a citizen enterprise in which we can educate each other rather than just be entertained.

I can't begin to imagine the many reasons why you and others are reading this book, but I hope that in the reading I have given you additional reasons why our present circumstance is ripe for something of our own making, instead of whatever the stakeholders of top-down government have in mind. I hope my argument has provided some nourishing food for thought that you can digest and then use in whatever ways make sense to you and those you share the journey with.

Notes

Introduction

1. Matt Bai adds another wrinkle: "There is after all, a short distance between believing that government doesn't solve our problems to believing that government actually causes them." "Obama, the Oil Spill and the Chaos Perception," *New York Times*, June 4, 2010. After the Tucson violence in early 2011, Bai focused on the "emergence of a political culture in blogs and Twitter and cable television—that so loudly reinforces the dark visions of political extremists often for profit or political gain." "A Turning Point in the Discourse, But in Which Direction," *New York Times,* January 9, 2011.

2. This very much reflects the cable news personalities who grab for our attention. Matt Bai sees such personalities as diminishing "the more mundane existence" of those in the government trenches to the point where we think "the gloss of entertainers and bullies is strangely more admirable." "Cable Guise," *New York Times,* December 6, 2009. David Brooks, so often on the mark, has written: "Now we seem to expect perfection from government and then throw temper tantrums when it is not. We seem to be in a position of young adolescents who believe mommy and daddy can take care of everything, and then grow angry and cynical when it becomes clear they can't." *New York Times,* Op/Ed, January 1, 2010. In a later piece when opining from London, Brooks commends Prime Minister David Cameron, whose government is "trying to get the British people to change their social norms. . . . Cameron says: Get off the couch and take responsibility for your community." *New York Times,* May 19, 2011.

3. Michael Emmer, "Complaint Box/Weather Forecasts," *New York Times* (City Room Blog) December 11, 2009. More than 25 years ago, Neil Postman saw it coming—television "has made entertainment itself the natural format for the presentation of all experience." Neil Postman, *Amusing Ourselves to Death: Public Discourse in the Age of Show Business* (Penguin Books, 1985), 87.

4. Mancur Olson, *The Logic of Collective Action: Public Goods and the Theory of Groups* (Harvard University Press, 1980), 105.

5. Robert Bellah et al., *The Good Society* (Knopf, 1991), 273.

6. What makes a problem is the difference between the way something is and the way we would prefer it to be. Karl Weick, *Sensemaking in Organizations* (Sage Publications, 1995), 8.

7. James Surowiecki, *The Wisdom of Crowds: Why the Many Are Smarter Than the Few and How Collective Wisdom Shapes Business, Economics, Societies, and Nations* (Doubleday, 2004), 271.

8. Daniel Boorstin, *Democracy and Its Discontents: Reflections on Everyday America* (Random House, 1974), 121.

9. Weick, *Sensemaking*, 31.

10. Parker Palmer from personal correspondence.

11. E. B. White, searchquotes.com/E_B_White/. . ./quotes/.

12. Richard Rorty, *Achieving Our Country: Leftist Thought in Twentieth-Century America* (Harvard University Press, 1998), 101. To paraphrase Jon Elster, my book is meant to have explanatory power about the ways things happen without predictive power of what will happen next. Jon Elster, *Nuts and Bolts for the Social Sciences* (Cambridge University Press, 1989), 8. Although I spent 20 years in the academy of higher education, I am not an academic. I prefer the moniker that Ed Koch once gave me: "a working intellectual." Daniel Bell made the distinction clear when he noted that an academic "has a bounded field of knowledge, a tradition, and seeks to find his place in it." The intellectual, Bell noted, "begins with *his* experience, *his* individual perceptions of the world, *his* privileges and deprivations, and judges the world by these sensibilities." Michael T. Kaufman, "Daniel Bell, Ardent Appraiser of Power, Economics and Culture, Dies at 91," *New York Times*, January 25, 2011.

Chapter 1

1. Charles Lindblom, *Inquiry and Change: The Troubled Attempt to Shape Society* (Yale University Press, 1990), 6.

2. John Stuart Mill, *On Liberty* (Appleton-Century-Crofts, Inc., 1947), 112.

3. Irving Howe said it is healthy, though confusing, to have more special interests rather than fewer. "Special Interest Cant," *New York Times*, March 8, 1984.

4. The criterion for who are lobbyists is whether they are getting paid to do so, "contacting public officials about a client's interests at least twice in a [calendar] quarter and working at least 20 percent of the time on lobby-related activities." David D. Kirkpatrick, "Law to Curb Lobbying Sends It Underground," *New York Times*, January 18, 2010.

5. Mancur Olson, *The Rise and Decline of Nations: Economic Growth, Stagflation, and Social Rigidities* (Yale University Press, 1982), 37. Academics

call this "rent seeking" where the cost to individual taxpayers is negligible but the benefit to certain special interests is considerable.

6. "Seeking predictability also means wanting a measure of control through centralized hierarchy in which experts retain more leverage to influence decision makers." For Steven Brint, "these preferences encourage a dismissive view of policy alternatives involving decentralization, dehierarchization, democratized participation." Steven Brint, *In an Age of Experts: The Changing Roles of Professionals in Politics and Public Life* (Princeton University Press, 1994), 146. "[P]recise scientific or theoretical formulations are as much a threat . . . as are the facile stories and instant analyses of the mass media." 211. They should, however, heed the words of Vaclev Havel: "The essence of life is infinitely and mysteriously multiform, and therefore it cannot be contained or planned for in its fullness and variability by any central intelligence." Quoted in John McMillan, *Reinventing the Bazaar: A Natural History of Markets* (W. W. Norton, 2002), 7.

7. Experts manipulate symbols to "solve, identify, and broker problems. . . . Their tools may be mathematical algorithms, legal arguments, financial gimmicks, scientific principles, psychological insights . . . or any other set of techniques for doing conceptual puzzles." Robert B. Reich, *The Work of Nations: Preparing Ourselves for 21st-Century Capitalism* (Vintage Books, 1992), 178.

8. Lindblom, *Inquiry and Change*, 276–277, footnote 35.

9. John Holland, *Hidden Order: How Adaptation Builds Complexity* (Addison Wesley, 1995), 11. Some experts, however, do use simulations in trying to reproduce some semblance of the complexities they are dealing with. Simulation models overcome one of the handicaps of policy analysis models which too often assume centralized solutions because they are easier to trace and track. Simulation models come closer and can remain truer to what actually may happen than the projections of more static models that are designed to control and thus overdetermine outcomes.

10. Alfred North Whitehead, *Science and the Modern World* (Free Press, 1967), 197. Certainly, not all professional advice givers are captives of their respective disciplines and methodologies. We encounter some of them among the doctors, lawyers, and financial advisers we seek out and who pursue a trial-and-error approach similar to our own when trying to figure out what to do about a particular problem. A useful analogy is the trial and error that a medical doctor pursues. She makes a tentative diagnosis and prescribes tentative treatment interventions to see what works and doesn't work. She wants more information, more feedback, more time. Prescription quantities are limited, dosages are adjusted, side effects are observed.

11. Alexis de Tocqueville, *Democracy in America*, ed. J.P. Mayer (Doubleday, 1969), 692.

12. James C. Scott raises a troubling point about the dominance of experts in statecraft. "If a planned social order is better than the accidental, irrational

deposit of historical practice . . . only those who have the scientific knowledge to discern and create this superior social order are fit to rule in the new age." Scott, *Seeing Like a State: How Certain Schemes to Improve the Human Condition Have Failed* (Yale University Press, 1998), 94. Yet as Charles Lindblom foresaw, the fall of communism and its planned social order was not necessarily a desire for liberty or the practice of democracy as it was the failure of intelligence in social organization. Lindblom, *Politics and Markets: The World's Political-Economic Systems* (Basic Books, 1997), 248.

13. Charles L. Lindblom and David K. Cohen, *Usable Knowledge: Social Science and Social Problem Solving* (Yale University Press, 1979), 10, 12, 15.

14. Anthony Flint, *Wrestling with Moses: How Jane Jacobs Took on New York's Master Builder and Transformed the American City* (Random House, 2009), 23. Flint offers the example of the Lower Manhattan Expressway in New York City, which fortunately was never built. The professional planners saw the neighborhoods affected by the proposed project as "blighted and so a highway should go through it; but the neighborhood was blighted because the city planned to put a highway through it." 164.

15. "As the client advances, the citizen retreats." John McKnight, "Do No Harm," *Social Policy* 20, no. 1 (Summer 1989): 7.

16. The final version of Boyte's essay is titled "Public Work: Civic Populism versus Technocracy in Higher Education," in *Agent of Democracy: Higher Education and the HEX Journey,* ed. David W. Brown and Deborah Witte (Kettering Foundation Press, 2008), 79–102.

17. David W. Brown, *When Strangers Cooperate: Using Social Conventions to Govern Ourselves* (Free Press, 1995), 122. All references to the author's previous works are cited under the name David W. Brown.

18. David H. Freedman, *Wrong: Why Experts* Keep Failing Us and How to Know When Not to Trust Them: Scientists, Finance Wizards, Doctors, Relationship Gurus, Celebrity CEOs, High-Powered Consultants, Health Officials, and More* (Little, Brown, 2010), 11.

19. Alex Jones, *Losing the News: The Future of the News That Feeds Democracy* (Oxford University Press, 2009), 3. "Opinion sells. And opinion is, relatively speaking, cheaper than news." 99. According to another observer, "more and more, Americans watch and read the news that fits their political proclivities and ignore the other side." Bill Bishop, *The Big Sort: Why the Clustering of Like-Minded Americans Is Tearing Us Apart* (Houghton Mifflin, 2008), 36. Bishop attributes much of this shift to the "unprecedented media choices" couch potato citizens now have, permitting them to "self-segregate into their own media communities." 74.

20. Philip Tetlock, *Expert Political Judgment: How Good Is It? How Can We Know?* (Princeton University Press, 2005), 119, 186.

21. David Freedman, *Wrong*, 150. The media "exist to get us to read about, watch, and listen to them, and that often means selecting and presenting expert findings in a way that is entertaining, provocative, and useful sounding."

22. Robert Darnton, *The Case for Books: Past, Present, and Future* (Public Affairs, 2009), 25. A quarter century before Darnton, Neil Postman pointed out that "most of our daily news is inert consisting of information that gives us something to talk about but cannot lead to any meaningful action." Postman, *Amusing Ourselves to Death* (Penguin Books, 1985), 68. Stories are for reading and listening to primarily.

23. David W. Brown, *Organization Smarts: Portable Skills for Professionals Who Want to Get Ahead* (Amacom, 2002), 123. Darnton, *The Case for Books*, 25. "Ask anyone involved in a reported happening. They will tell you that they did not recognize themselves in the story that appeared in the paper." When we ask, "what's your take on what happened," we acknowledge how many different ways a mix of events can be remembered, interpreted, and summarized. Of course, I became and become a storyteller here, too, since neither I nor anyone else knows for sure everything about any particular incident.

24. Karl Weick, the social psychologist, argues, "Efforts to maintain the illusion that organizations are rational and orderly in the interest of *legitimacy* are costly and futile." Weick, *Making Sense of the Organization* (Blackwell Publishers, 2001), xi.

25. I have always liked Bob Behn's characterization of this behavior as "groping along." Robert D. Behn, "Management by Groping Along," *Journal of Policy Analysis and Management* 7, no. 4 (1988): 643–663.

26. It reminds me of Mario Vargas Llosa's observation about New York City. "The motley variety of the city, which cannot be assimilated to any single way of belief, thought or action; a Babel-like city, multiracial and multicultural, a miniature refraction of humanity's infinite variety." "Out of Many, New York," *New York Times,* Op-Ed, December 11, 2001.

27. Duncan Watts makes much the same point in *Six Degrees: The Science of a Connected Age* (W. W. Norton, 2003), 14–15. Watts writes about "doing science." "[B]y the time it gets out into the larger social world and everyone reads about it in books, it has been so reworked and refined that it takes on an aura of inevitability it never had in the making." Watts sees clearly how we confer honor and credit to those who may not deserve it. Watts call this "iconification" that can mislead our intuition when we try to understand the origins of collective, as opposed to individual, behavior." 247. The "collective," the "we," often gets short shrift by those egos in power whose stories leave *us* out.

28. Adam Nagourney and Jeff Zeleny, "Obama Formally Enters Presidential Race," *New York Times*, February 11, 2007.

29. "The idea was to transform Obama's list of activists and small dollar contributors into a neighborhood-by-neighborhood organization that could be mobilized to support his policy agenda." Matt Bai, "Democrat in Chief," *New York Times Magazine*, June 7, 2010.

30. Howard Dean's 2004 campaign for his party's nomination probably came closest to an investment in public work beyond political strings tied to a national agenda. Dean on reflection saw that "supporters didn't just raise

money; they formed service corps and volunteer projects to make donations to food banks and clothing drives, to deliver toys to needy kids at Christmas." Howard Dean, "How the Web is Restoring Democracy to Politics," forbes.com/forbes/2007/0507/094.html.

31. "Americans have often placed their faith in either the market or government regulation switching angrily from one to the other after inevitable disappointment, while giving relatively little attention to the development of social cooperation beyond the local level." William Sullivan, *Work and Integrity: The Crisis and Promise of Professionalism in America* (Harper Collins, 1995), 189. David Bornstein puts it succinctly that we have learned from a long record of failures that governments "are not necessarily the most effective vehicles, and certainly not the sole legitimate vehicles, for the actual delivery of many social goods, and they are often less inventive than entrepreneurial citizen organizations." Bornstein, *How to Change the World: Social Entrepreneurs and the Power of New Ideas* (Oxford University Press, 2004), 8.

32. Matthew A. Crenson and Benjamin Ginsberg, *Downsizing Democracy: How America Sidelined Its Citizens and Privatized Its Public* (Johns Hopkins University Press, 2004), 203. The authors, however, make an important point that less hierarchical forms of government have given citizens more access to government but mainly as individuals, and "decentralized and privatized" non-hierarchical policies have "atomized into thousands of market transactions" that "are not conducive to widespread collective mobilization." 202.

33. To his credit, Harry Truman did once concede as much. Truman felt sorry for his successor in the White House, Dwight Eisenhower. "He'll say, 'Do this! Do that! And nothing will happen." Richard E. Neustadt, *Presidential Power and the Modern Presidents: The Politics of Leadership* (John Wiley, 1960), 9.

Chapter 2

1. David Brooks sides with Leo Tolstoy who believed that "the everyday experiences of millions of people . . . organically and chaotically shape the destiny of nations—from the bottom up. . . . Societies move and breathe on their own, through the jostling of mentalities and habits." David Brooks, "Heroes and History," *New York Times,* July 17, 2007. David Bornstein also offers a positive perspective: "[M]ore people today have the freedom, time, wealth, health, exposure, social mobility, and confidence to address social problems in bold new ways." For Bornstein, the conditions for survival and self-interest have relaxed as compared to earlier periods of our history. David Bornstein, *How to Change the World* (Oxford University Press, 2004), 7.

2. Eva Braun, *Paradoxes of Education in a Republic* (University of Chicago Press, 1979), 2.

3. Many social outcomes become conventions that we take for granted. Conventions are defined as "regularities of behavior sustained by an interest in coordination and an expectation that others will do their part." David Lewis, *Convention: A Philosophical Study* (Harvard University Press, 1969), 208.

4. David W. Brown, *When Strangers Cooperate: Using Social Conventions to Govern Ourselves* (Free Press, 1995), 24.

5. Jane Jacobs, *The Death and Life of Great American Cities* (Vintage Books, 1961), 31–32.

6. William H. Whyte, *City: Rediscovering the Center* (Anchor Books, 1988), 67.

7. Brown, *When Strangers Cooperate*, 66. Throughout the world, there are other common pool resource undertakings such as inshore fisheries, grazing areas, groundwater basins, and communal forests—renewable resources where substantial scarcity exists. Eleanor Ostrom, *Governing the Commons: The Evolution of Institutions for Collective Action* (Cambridge University Press, 1990), 26.

8. Luis Alberto Urrea, "Kankakee Gets Its Groove Back," *New York Times,* Op-Ed, June 11, 2006.

9. Slug-lines.com.

10. Micky Sadoff, *America Gets MADD* (Mothers Against Drunk Driving, 1990).

11. City Harvest 2007 Annual Report.

12. I would make the comparison of social change with biological evolution: "Life is always poised for flight. From a distance, it looks still . . . but up close it is flitting this way and that, as if displaying to the world at every moment its perpetual readiness to take off in any of a thousand directions." Douglas H. Chadwick's review of Jonathan Weiner's *The Beak of the Finch, New York Times Book Review*, May 22, 1994.

13. Happenstance is explained this way: "Like . . . seedlings in a crowded plot of ground: whichever is the first to show vigorous growth can stifle the others." Robert Sugden, *The Economics of Rights, Co-operation, and Welfare* (Basil Blackwell, 1986), 43.

14. Allison Fine, *Momentum: Igniting Social Change in the Connected Age* (Jossey-Bass, 2006), 84.

15. David W. Brown, "Professional Virtue," *Change,* November/December 1985, 8; Jacques Barzun, *Teacher in America* (Liberty Press, 1981), 386.

16. David W. Brown, "The Journey of a Recovering Professional," *Higher Education Exchange,* 2008, 10–11. I should also note that what I learned about problem solving in my classrooms semester after semester and year after year was the example of women in their respective working groups helping the group work—together. Such experience prompts me to foresee the critical role that women can play in changing the current culture of professionalism who are prepared "to reject or modify the professional mind-set that currently educates

them, hires them, and evaluates them—a mind-set predominately crafted by men for men in times past" when women did not have the opportunities they do today. I think the century-old story of what it means to be professional is bound to change when altered and enlarged by the example of women. Ibid., 10.

17. Dennis Chong, *Collective Action and the Civil Rights Movement* (University of Chicago Press, 1991), 134.

18. Claude S. Fischer, *Made in America: A Social History of American Culture and Character* (University of Chicago Press, 2010), 42.

19. Victor D. Brooks, *Boomers: The Cold-War Generation Grows Up* (Ivan R. Dee, 2009), 146.

20. Malcolm Gladwell, *The Tipping Point: How Little Things Can Make a Big Difference* (Little, Brown, 2000), 7.

21. There are those who have analyzed emergence in the social context of like-minded people finding each other, after which small self-organized communities form, and then the common work of such communities scales up in no predictable way eventually becoming the norm for others to imitate, follow, join. Margaret Wheatley and Deborah Frieze, "Using Emergence to Take Social Innovations to Scale," *Kettering Review* (Summer 2009): 34–38.

22. David Brooks sees the "passion" of the movement and argues that "American history is often driven by passionate outsiders who force themselves into the center of American life." *New York Times,* Op-Ed, January 5, 2010.

23. Francesca Polletta, *It Was Like a Fever: Storytelling in Protest and Politics* (University of Chicago Press, 2006), 10–11.

24. John Holland uses the analogy of chess pieces which "interact to support one another." You can't simply add the value of each piece. If properly arranged they can "overwhelm an opponent with higher-valued pieces that are poorly arrayed." John Holland, *Emergence: From Chaos to Order* (Addison Wesley, 1998), 14.

25. Philip Slater, *The Pursuit of Loneliness: American Culture at the Breaking Point* (Beacon Press, 1970), 4.

26. Cass Sunstein, "Social Norms and Social Rules," *Columbia Law Review* (1996): 930.

27. Dan Kemmis, *The Good City and the Good Life: Renewing the Sense of Community* (Houghton Mifflin, 1995), 201.

28. Matt Ridley, *The Origins of Virtue: Human Instincts and the Evolution of Cooperation* (Viking, 1996), 181.

29. Chong, *Collective Action and the Civil Rights Movement,* 36.

30. Ibid., 84–85, citing Howell Raines, *My Soul Is Rested: Movement Days in the Deep South Remembered* (G. P. Putnam's Sons, 1977) 44–45.

31. James A. Morone, *The Democratic Wish: Popular Participation and the Limits of American Government,* rev. ed. (Yale University Press, 1998), 142.

32. William Galston, "A Liberal Democratic Case for the Two Parent Family" *The Responsive Community* (Winter 1990–1991): 14–26, 15.

33. Richard Flacks, *Making History: The American Left and the American Mind* (Columbia University Press, 1988), 83.

34. Paul Hawken, a leading commentator on the environmental movement, sees three "basic roots: environmental activism, social justice initiatives and indigenous cultures' resistance to globalization, all of which have become intertwined." Paul Hawken, *Blessed Unrest: How the Largest Movement in the World Came into Being and Why No One Saw It Coming* (Viking, 2007), 12. Hawken argues that such a movement can never be centralized "because no single ideology can ever heal the wounds of the world." 163.

35. Clay Shirky, *Here Comes Everybody: The Power of Organizing without Organizations* (Penguin Press, 2008), 20–21.

Chapter 3

1. Mitchell Resnick, *Turtles, Termites, and Traffic Jams: Explorations in Massively Parallel Microworlds* (MIT Press, 1994), 8.

2. Chris Anderson, *The Long Tail: Why the Future of Business Is Selling Less of More* (Hyperion, 2006), 6.

3. Michael Sandel, "Political Theory of the Procedural Republic," in *The Power of Public Ideas*, ed. Robert Reich (Bellinger, 1988), 120.

4. Jeffrey Kluger argues that "all of us have a tendency to believe that the rest of the group knows what it's doing." Jeffrey Kluger, *Simplexity: Why Simple Things Become Complex (and How Complex Things Can Be Made Simple)* (Hyperion, 2008), 53. Joining the crowd, which makes a crowd, is also one reason for a highway speed limit, which coordinates our driving behavior. The actual speed limit, 55, 65, or 75 mph, is less important than a maximum speed, which makes driver behavior more predictable. What creates dangerous driving conditions is the behavior of those whose speed varies significantly with what enough others are doing. Charles A. Lave, "Speeding, Coordination and the 55 mph Speed Limit," *American Economic Review* (December, 1985), 1159–1164, 1159.

5. Deborah Stone, *The Samaritan's Dilemma: Should Government Help Your Neighbor?* (Nation Books, 2008), 234–235.

6. David Lewis, *Convention: A Philosophic Study* (Harvard University Press, 1969), 88. Lewis also compares the quickening development and momentum to getting caught up in "fashions, fads, panics, riots and bandwagons." 121.

7. Alexis de Tocqueville, *Democracy in America* (Anchor Book, 1969), 515.

8. Theodore Roszak, *The Making of an Elder Culture: Reflections on the Future of America's Most Audacious Generation* (New Society Publishers, 2009), 92.

9. Michael Taylor, "Rationality and Revolutionary Collective Action," in *Rationality and Revolution,* ed. Michael Taylor, Studies in Marxism and Social

Theory (Cambridge University Press, 1982), 84. When your local co-members call on you, it's harder to ignore or decline their requests. On the other hand, size counts in another way—the larger the member base, the more likely the NGO will reap sizable sums from a few large contributors. Pamela Oliver and Gerald Maxwell, "The Paradox of Group Size in Collective Action: A Theory of the Critical Mass II," *Sociological Review*, 53 (1988): 1–8, 6.

10. Bill Schambra put it well: "[T]hey have a map of the problem in their head, and a map of the solution so that no matter how open-ended they say they are to community input, that's all it is, is community input." Cynthia Gibson, "Citizens at the Center," *Case Foundation* (2006): 23. The motion is seconded by Allison Fine: "[M]embers and volunteers . . . enthusiastically embrace [NGO campaigns and programs] after the fact . . . into which they had no input." *Momentum* (Jossey-Bass, 2006), 5. There are exceptions, of course, like the Industrial Area Foundation that never does anything for those who can do it for themselves. The IAF seeks to build capacity rather than render service. The Texas IAF and the Southwest IAF are models of something that has proved enduring. The IAF networks normally have 20–60 member affiliate organizations reaching roughly one million families through 2000 church congregations, schools, and other organizations—a membership-network on the ground that remains "one of America's premier experiments in reviving democracy." Mark R. Warren, *Dry Bones Rattling: Community Building to Revitalize American Democracy* (Princeton University Press, 2001), 7. These networks "see democracy within the group as vital to building democracy outside it." Francesca Polletta, *Freedom Is an Endless Meeting* (University of Chicago Press, 2002), 177.

11. John Javna, Sophie Javna, and Jesse Javna, *50 Simple Things You Can Do to Save the Earth* (Hyperion, 2008).

12. Theda Skocpol, *Diminshed Democracy: From Membership to Management in American Civic Life* (University of Oklahoma Press, 2003), 149, 163, and 207.

13. Ibid., 227.

14. Richard C. Harwood and John A. Creighton, "The Organization-First Approach," Harwood Institute for Public Innovation, 2009, 2–18.

15. David W. Brown, *When Strangers Cooperate: Using Social Conventions to Govern Ourselves* (Free Press, 1995), 62.

16. Thomas C. Schelling, *Micromotives and Macrobehavior* (W. W. Norton, 1978), 251.

17. Robert F. Worth, "Opposition in Iran Meets a Crossroads on Strategy," *New York Times* (February 15, 2010).

18. John Seely Brown and Paul Duguid, *The Social Life of Information* (Harvard Business School Press, 2002), xiii. Others, too, warn us of the harmless but wasteful use of the Internet. "The Internet is a picture not of our life but of our dream world, where each of us is a little emperor of appetite and opinion and everyone has to listen." Adam Gopnick, *Through the Children's Gate* (Knopf, 2006), 297. "Social networking [My Space, Facebook, etc.] . . . in

reality they exist so that we can advertise ourselves." Andrew Keen, *The Cult of the Amateur: How Today's Internet Is Killing Our Culture* (Doubleday/Currency, 2007), 7.

19. Clay Shirky hits the mark when he says "much of what gets posted on any given day is in public but not for the public." Clay Shirky, *Here Comes Everybody: The Power of Organizing without Organizations* (Penguin Press, 2008), 90. In a subsequent book, however, Shirky holds out hope for the young generation who are shifting from TV to social media, which includes engagement with others, not just consumption. They can produce and share with each other. *Cognitive Surplus: Creativity and Generosity in a Connected Age* (Penguin Press, 2010), 11 and 22.

20. Jason Lanier, *You Are Not a Gadget: A Manifesto* (Knopf, 2010), 20.

21. John McMillan made the apt comparison of the Internet to a market economy both with their "decentralized structure and freewheeling nature." McMillan, *Reinventing the Bazaar: A Natural History of Markets* (W. W. Norton, 2002), 155. The Internet also has an "open structure" which allows it "to develop not by plan but by evolution." 156. Even Robert Putnam, who badly erred on the side of traditional groups in explaining the decline of "social capital," acknowledged that the growth of the Internet was a hopeful trend along with the grass root activities of "evangelical conservatives, the increase in self-help support groups and the rise of youth volunteering." Putnam, *Bowling Alone: The Collapse and Revival of American Community* (Simon & Schuster, 2000), 180. Still, Putnam thought the Internet is better "at maintaining communities already formed, they are less good at making them." 18. An unqualified appreciation of the Internet came from David Bornstein and his ambitious look at social entrepreneurs and their use of the Internet. For Bornstein, "people [now] possess powerful communication tools to coordinate efforts to attack [social] problems such as health care, education and poverty." David Bornstein, *How to Change the World* (Oxford University Press, 2004), 7.

22. Anderson, *Long Tail,* 99.

23. Michael Sandel, *Democracy's Discontent: America in Search of a Public Philosophy* (Belknap/Harvard University Press, 1996), 340.

24. Theda Skocpol sees evangelical churches with perhaps the broadest and most active memberships. Megachurches have become communities themselves, especially where exurbia provides little support or social centeredness. Skocpol goes on to take issue with putting much reliance on secular membership federations, arguing that in this vast country they have not marshaled great influence because they lack ties to those with political power. *Diminished Democracy,* 256. That certainly can't be said for the evangelical influence in national politics.

25. John McKnight, *The Careless Society: Community and Its Counterfeits* (Basic Books, 1995), 165. Some argue, however, that NGOs help make whatever time volunteers offer more efficient. Macedo et al., *Democracy at Risk* (Brookings Institution Press, 2005), 123.

26. Cathy Monroe, "Brown Colors Blackburn with Community Spirit," *State Journal-Register*, September 14, 1989, 21.

27. Robert Wuthnow, *Loose Connections: Joining Together in America's Fragmented Communities* (Harvard University Press, 1998), 88. Other commentators use the term "convoy." We travel through our lives in social convoys with those we are acquainted with in one way or another and who become resources from time to time as the need arises. Melinda Blau and Karen L. Fingerman, *Consequential Strangers: The Power of People Who Don't Seem to Matter . . . but Really Do* (W. W. Norton, 2009), 8. There are many groups evolving, however, which sit somewhere between member organizations and those with only loose connections. They include affinity groups, workshops, consciousness-raising groups, residential clusters, and the workplace itself. Francesca Polletta, *Freedom Is an Endless Meeting*, 222.

28. Mark S. Granovetter, "The Strength of Weak Ties," *American Journal of Sociology* 8, no. 6 (1973): 1360–1379. Granovetter argued long before Robert Wuthnow that having many "weak ties" to others helped "diffuse what is involved" 1367, and "more people can be reached." 1369. More recently, Paul Seabright sums well the weak ties argument in *The Company of Strangers: A Natural History of Economic Life* (Princeton University Press, 2004), 64–65. And Richard Florida adds a wrinkle by noting that those who share similar lifestyle preferences in some urban settings establish new social ties without regard to particular neighborhoods *per se*, and they prefer quasi *anonymity*, which means living their own life and being themselves. *The Rise of the Creative Class: And How It's Transforming Work, Leisure, Community, and Everyday Life* (Basic Books, 2002), 269. Moreover, Claude Fischer sees a long-standing circumstance of Americans choosing their communities, not just inheriting them. *Made in America: A Social History of American Culture and Character* (University of Chicago Press, 2010), 98. This has certainly been true of those who have left the church denomination of their childhood for a new church membership of their own choosing. Ibid., 154.

29. "Outbreeding," an analogy of weak ties, as opposed to "inbreeding," has been rewarding in evolutionary history. David Mindell makes the point that "diversity tends to beget more diversity" and "species-rich ecosystems tend to be more stable and productive" over time. *The Evolving World: Evolution in Everyday Life* (Harvard University Press, 2006), 194. Weak social ties begetting more diversity have the potential to be more productive too. Facebook serves as an inventory "of our social connections, especially our weak ties." Blau and Fingerman, *Consequential Strangers*, 35.

30. Jacobs, *The Death and Life of Great American Cities*, 82.

31. Matthew A. Crenson and Benjamin Ginsberg, *Downsizing Democracy: How America Sidelined Its Citizens and Privatized Its Public* (Johns Hopkins University Press, 2002), 18.

32. In another context describing "ecologies of knowledge" in Silicon Valley, John Seely Brown and Paul Duguid argue that an "ecology at large is an

enormously powerful, significantly self-organizing ecosystem developing new ideas ubiquitously." *The Social Life of Information,* 172. So it is with any network where social attention and self-organizing can originate and develop.

33. Sara M. Evans and Harry C. Boyte, *Free Spaces: The Sources of Democratic Change in America* (Harper & Row, 1986), 17. Even top-down government has thought of new ways to create public space online to include citizens marginally as it pursues its agenda. Federal agencies have created digital public space for soliciting citizen ideas and allowing them to vote on each other's proposals. One such "crowd source" effort, however, was characterized as "embarrassing" when out of 44,000 proposals the one that got the most votes was the legalization of marijuana. I don't think that is embarrassing, but it does show that such one-shot crowd sourcing may be of questionable value. The legalization of marijuana is a request made to top-down government with very little effort otherwise needed on the part of those responding. Anand Giridharadas, " 'Athens' on the Net," *New York Times,* September 13, 2009.

34. Fischer, *Made in America,* 162, 9.

35. David W. Brown, "Public Grieving and Public Thinking," *Higher Education Exchange,* 2002, 6.

36. Those with credentials produce outcomes which are rarely solutions given the ceaseless flow of events that make and remake outcomes without end. An outcome more closely resembles an equilibrium, or as deftly phrased by one observer, "what is there after something has settled down, if something ever does settle down." Schelling, *Micromotives and Macrobehavior,* 26.

37. Richard M. Merelman, *Making Something of Ourselves: On Culture and Politics in the United States* (University of California Press, 1984), 243.

38. Deborah Stone, *The Samaritan's Dilemma,* 274. And Claude Fischer expands the list to "bartering, exchanging labor, managing commons, mounting a militia, providing emergency care. . . ." *Made in America,* 103.

39. Malcolm Gladwell, *Outliers: The Story of Success* (Little, Brown, 2008), 33.

40. Putnam, *Bowling Alone,* 40. Putnam was speaking of political giving but the same can be said for NGO support. Not enough *time* is so often the excuse. It reminds me of the often-cited objection, attributed to Oscar Wilde, that socialism would take up too many evenings. Quoted in Michael Walzer's *Obligations: Essays on Disobedience, War, and Citizenship* (Harvard University Press, 1970), 230.

41. Albert O. Hirschman, *Exit, Voice, Loyalty: Responses to Decline in Firms, Organizations, and States* (Harvard University Press, 1970), 65.

42. Americans have always moved on, if not away from problems then looking for a new start with new opportunities someplace else. Claude Fischer notes that poverty has always been a very good reason to move on. "As late as the early 1900s, about half of American families could be classified as poor, and they moved around frequently." Fischer offers the example that 75 percent of Pittsburgh residents in 1900 were not there in 1905. *Made in America,* 47.

43. Richard Flacks notes that such experience can be invaluable in a new undertaking. *Making History: The American Left and the American Mind* (Columbia University Press, 1988), 73.

44. David W. Brown, *Organization Smarts: Portable Skills for Professionals Who Want to Get Ahead* (Amacom, 2002), 190.

45. Charles Lindblom and David K. Cohen describe "social learning" as an "actual experience that upsets old attitudes and dispositions." *Usable Knowledge: Social Science and Social Problem Solving* (Yale University Press, 1979), 18. As they put it: "Things will have to get worse before they can get better." 19. What they mean is that we won't really do much to make a situation better until we experience its consequences and resolve to correct them. Consider the experience of unemployment. In normal times, we may read about it and think of it as an unfortunate statistic but little more. In the recent serious recession that smacked almost everyone in some way, unemployment too often became your problem or a family member's problem.

46. I recall Jane Jacobs's efforts in Greenwich Village where the naming of committees was meant to reflect the immediacy of a threat and the urgency to take action such as "The Joint Emergency Committee to Close Washington Square to Traffic" or "The Committee to Get the Clock Started on the Jefferson Market Courthouse." Jacobs wanted to be sure that "[p]eople knew what they were getting into. They weren't getting into ideology. They were getting into a particular thing." Anthony Flint, *Wrestling with Moses: How Jane Jacobs Took on New York's Master Builder and Transformed the American City* (Random House, 2009), 79.

47. Shirky, *Cognitive Surplus*, 186.

48. Albert O. Hirschman, *Shifting Involvements: Private Interest and Public Action* (Princeton University Press, 1982), 89.

49. Deborah Stone even argues that praising others as "altruistic" leads them to believe they are and they may act accordingly. *The Samaritan's Dilemma*, 198.

50. Shirky, *Cognitive Surplus*, 77.

51. Clay Shirky thinks of such flexibility as establishing "the pattern of collaborative circles," not pursuing a "master strategy but instead open to "broad experimentation." *Cognitive Surplus*, 186. Richard Rorty makes much the same point: "When we see this community as *ours* rather than nature's shaped rather than found, one among many that men have made. . . . [W]hat matters is our loyalty to other human beings clinging together against the dark, not our hope of getting things right." Richard Rorty, *Consequences of Pragmatism: Essays, 1972–1980* (University of Minnesota Press, 1982), 166.

52. Brown, *When Strangers Cooperate*, 124.

53. I discussed the problems of success in a monograph, David W. Brown, "Cooperation Among Strangers," An Occasional Paper of the Kettering Foundation (1992), 30.

Chapter 4

1. Jackson Lears, *No Place of Grace* (Pantheon Books, 1981), 306. Richard Merleman also saw that "the liberated individual, not the social group," emerged. *Making Something of Ourselves: On Culture and Politics in the United States* (University of California Press, 1984), 30.

2. David W. Brown, "Professional Virtue," *Change* (November/December 1985), 9.

3. Dan Barry, "Boomers Hit New Self-Absorption Milestone: Age 65," *New York Times*, December 31, 2010.

4. "As late as 1870, people sixty-five years or older were only one of every thirty-three Americans; in the early 2000s, they composed about one in eight Americans; in 2050, they will probably be one in *five*." Claude S. Fischer, *Made in America* (University of Chicago Press, 2010), 28. David Brooks captured the contradiction the Boomers confront: "In the private sphere . . . seniors provide wonderful gifts for their grandchildren, loving attention that will linger in young minds, providing support for decades to come. In the public sphere, they take it away." David Brooks, "The Geezers' Crusade," *New York Times*, February 2, 2010.

5. There are already many models for bestowing attention on and care for others. One example is Senior Corps, a program of the Federal Corporation for National and Community Service. Recently, Senior Corps has sought out more Boomers to be companions to the elderly helping them with shopping and medical appointments, and as foster grandparents who mentor youth. aarp.org/bulletin Jan–Feb 2011, 18 (removed from website). Workplace wellness programs have also sought to improve the health of their employees, increase productivity, and reduce employer and employee health costs. A big percentage of the health costs that employers face are for employees with diabetes and hypertension that arise from bad eating habits. Ron Lieber, "Incentivize Your Way to Good Health," *New York Times*, December 31, 2010.

6. Paid advertisement, "Why Are We Subsidizing Childhood Obesity?" *New York Times*, October 26, 2010.

7. Jane Brody summarizes one dimension of the obesity problem. "Americans are now caught in a vicious cycle of increasing fatness, with prospective mothers starting out fatter, gaining more weight during pregnancy and giving birth to babies who are destined to become overweight adults." Jane Brody, "Weight Problems May Begin in the Womb," *New York Times*, September 6, 2010.

8. Joshua T. Cohen, Peter J. Neumann, and Milton C. Weinstein, "Does Preventive Care Save Money? Health Economics and the Presidential Candidates," *New England Journal of Medicine*, February 14, 2008, 661.

9. Natasha Sanger, "Eat an Apple (Doctor's Orders)," *New York Times*, August 12, 2010.

10. Many school districts are starting school gardens using local produce and getting parents involved in the planning of meals. info@messages. whitehouse.gov (December 15, 2010). Some parents are already going to their schools, finding out what is served, and looking at the school's wellness policy. Using leftovers and wholesome breads, some have resumed making lunches for their children to take with them.

11. Andrew Martin, "Government's Dietary Advice: Eat Less," *New York Times*, January 31, 2011.

12. Roni Caryn Rabin, "Obese American Spend Far More on Health Care," *New York Times*, July 28, 2009.

13. Anthony Flint, *Wrestling with Moses* (Random House, 2009), 193. The workplace is also getting attention. Sixty years ago, one of two Americans had a physically active job. Now only one of five do. Standing workstations, treadmill-style desks, and putting printers some distance from desks are just a few of the ways of addressing an overly sedentary work life routine. Tara Parker-Pope, "Workplace Cited as a New Source of Rise in Obesity," *New York Times*, May 26, 2011.

14. Jane Brody, "Risks for Youth Who Eat What They Watch," *New York Times*, April 19, 2010.

15. Sam Dolnick, "The Obesity-Hunger Paradox," *New York Times*, March 12, 2010.

16. One skeptical observer asked: "Can Michelle Obama make field greens and strawberries as comforting, satisfying and heartwarmingly American as apple pie? She has her work cut out for her." Judith Warner, "Junking Junk Food," *New York Times*, November 25, 2010. The community garden idea has also been pursued by the Tohono O'odham community in Arizona fighting a very high rate of diabetes. They have created two farms, market traditional foods once part of their diet, and provide them for sale in the community and to hospitals, schools, and elderly lunch programs. www.tocaonline.org. And there is the farmer to local market connection that can be strengthened, linking local food growers, process distributors, and retailers.

17. Michael Pollan, "Out of the Kitchen, onto the Couch," *New York Times*, August 2, 2009.

18. Michael Pollan, "Big Food v. Big Insurance," *New York Times*, September 10, 2009.

19. Gina Kolata, "Law May Do Little to Help Curb Unnecessary Care," *New York Times*, March 29, 2010.

20. Theodore Roszak, *The Making of an Elder Culture: Reflections on the Future of America's Most Audacious Generation* (New Society Publishers, 2009), 82.

21. Those who object to government meddling, by having to pay for others' bad habits, ignore their many opportunities to help others change those bad habits. Ironically, those who think that everyone should look after themselves

and who show no interest in helping others improve their health, end up with more government meddling, not less. "The whole point of insurance [whether it is private heath insurance or government-funded Medicaid and Medicare] is to reduce risk. When people inveigh against the lack of personal responsibility in health care, they are really demanding a different model, one based on actual risk, not just on spreading costs evenly through society. Sick people should pay more. Which model we eventually adopt in this country will say a lot about the kind of society we want to live in." Sandeep Jauhar, M.D., "No Matter What, We Pay for Others' Bad Habits," *New York Times*, March 29, 2010.

22. Philip K. Howard, "Health Reform's Taboo Topic," *Washington Post*, July 31, 2009.

23. Sandeep Jauhar, M.D., "Out of Camelot, Knights in White Coats Lose Their Way," *New York Times*, January 31, 2011.

24. Steve Lohr, "Adding Health Advice to Online Medical Records," *New York Times*, October 6, 2009.

25. LAMsight, a project of MIT's Media Lab, is an example of getting individuals to be sources for a database that can aggregate their inputs to assist in medical research. LAM, by the way, is short for lympangioleiomyomatosis, which is a predator of the lungs. Without an abbreviation, I'm not sure I would have the breath to pronounce it otherwise.

26. Melinda Blau and Karen L. Fingerman, *Consequential Strangers* (W. W. Norton, 2009), 98.

27. The Village to Village Network is a rapidly growing movement nationwide of local organizations whose members help their local elderly maintain independence despite the afflictions of aging. There is an annual fee in return for a variety of services. vtvnetwork.org. There is also an emerging technological effort to wire people up at home so that others can monitor their health status. Telehealth is not a perfect fix by any means, but when combined with those who can look in and look after the homebound and aged population, such monitoring can offer both remote and personal attention. There will surely be other new technologies for monitoring those who require licensed care with some of their needs being met by those without license but ready to help. Milt Freudenheim, "Wired Up at Home to Monitor Illnesses," *New York Times*, November 24, 2010.

28. Walker Smith and Ann Clurman, *Generation Ageless: How Baby Boomers Are Changing the Way We Live Today . . . and They're Just Getting Started* (Collins, 2007), 172 and Deborah Stone, *The Samaritan's Dilemma* (Nation Books, 2008), 103. According to a 2003 survey, 44 million people representing one-fifth of American adults were caregivers to other adults. The survey considered a caregiver as one who provides help with dressing, walking, paying bills, or shopping.

29. R. McClintock, studyplace.org/wiki/Defining_education/Prolegomenon. As my colleague, David Mathews, has said, let's "start with communities rather

than schools and start with education broadly defined rather than formal instruction." David Mathews, "The Public and the Public Schools: The Coproduction of Education," *Phi Delta Kappan*, April 2008.

30. Lawrence A. Cremin, *American Education: The Colonial Experience, 1607–1783* (Harper & Row, 1970), 192–193.

31. Lawrence A. Cremin, *American Education: The National Experience, 1783–1876* (Harper & Row, 1980), 266.

32. For Larry Cremin, "whatever else [TV] does . . . it educates and miseducates relentlessly. It conveys information and knowledge through programs and documentaries; it creates wants through commercials; and it offers models of behavior through soap operas and sitcoms." Lawrence A. Cremin, *Public Education* (Basic Books, 1976), 56.

33. Malcolm Gladwell, *Outliers: The Story of Success* (Little, Brown, 2008), 112–113.

34. www.oasiscenter.org, accessed April 27, 2011.

35. www.theinnovationcenter.org, accessed April 27, 2011.

36 www.nonviolentmen.org, accessed April 27, 2011.

37. Wick Sloane, from personal correspondence.

Another former graduate student where I taught has taken the lead to provide a multitude of intersections for the Boomer generation to get involved. Marc Freedman's work evolved from Experience Corps to Encore Careers, which encourages and facilitates service opportunities for those over 55 as tutors and mentors both in school and after school. www.encore.org, accessed April 28, 2011. In his most recent book, Freedman holds out new hope for his generation: "Instead of trying to be younger than we are, we need to accept our age and our stage and invest in those who are truly young." *The Big Shift: Navigating the New Stage beyond Midlife* (Public Affairs, 2011), 175.

38. Michael Sandel, *Liberalism and the Limits of Justice* (Cambridge University Press, 1982), 76.

39. Parker Palmer, *The Active Life: Wisdom of Work, Creativity and Caring* (Harper & Row, 1990), 134. The Amish community is off to one side in American life, but its culture is a precedent for what others can do. For the Amish, "Family and community serve as insurance, welfare, social security, public safety. Indeed, they serve as, and replace government." Wendell Berry, *The Unsettling of America* (Avon Books, 1977), 212.

40. David Owen, "The Efficiency Dilemma," *New Yorker*, December 20, 2010.

41. "City Harvest News" and "Annual Reports," 2006–2010.

42. Theodore Roszak recalled the "free store" that briefly existed in San Francisco during the 1967 Summer of Love, then thought of as a "countercultural improvisation" that offered food, household goods, and wearable clothing. Roszak, *Making of an Elder Culture*, 157. It reminds me of the individual homeowners in the New Hampshire town where we lived who would merely

place household items in their front yard near the curb with a sign reading "Free." "The world of altruism, far from being an economy of scarce resources and mine-or-thine, operates as an economy of abundance and mine-*and*-thine." Stone, *Samaritan's Dilemma*, 187.

43. Roszak, *Making of an Elder Culture*, 147.

44. Jim Dwyer, "Where Unsold Clothes Meet People in Need," *New York Times*, January 10, 2010.

45. Jim Dwyer, "From Deep in the Closet to a Needy Girl's Prom," *New York Times*, March 26, 2010.

46. www.communitygarden.org/learn/starting-a-community-garden.php, accessed April 28, 2011.

47. Smith and Clurman, *Generation Ageless*, 160.

48. Ibid., 33.

49. Hannah Pitkin, "Justice: On Relating Private and Public," *Political Theory* 9, no. 3 (1981): 337–351, 348.

50. Roszak, *Making of an Elder Culture*, 8 and 14.

51. Ibid., 207.

52. Ibid., 142

53. Ken Dychtwald, foreword to Richard Croker, *The Boomer Century: How America's Most Influential Generation Changed Everything* (Springboard Press, 2007), ix. Dychtwald goes on to say, "We have more time, money, and wisdom to contribute than any generation before us. How will we use these assets in the coming decades?" 305.

Chapter 5

1. Admittedly, there are always government policies and laws that go way beyond what we could manage to do together on our own. The GI Bill after World War II influenced the creation of postwar families, given the scale of the legislation's benefits that favored married veterans with children and had a direct bearing on the sheer numbers of Boomers who can still play a starring role on the citizen side of the street. Victor D. Brooks, *Boomers: The Cold War Generation Grows Up* (Ivan R. Dee, 2009), 20.

2. Anthony Flint credits Jane Jacobs's neighborhood work for helping to produce a culture change where "Everything from the design of workplaces to social media—the online networks of Facebook, YouTube, and open-source software—owes a debt to Jacobs and her original analysis of how decentralized, diverse, and ground-up systems function best." Anthony Flint, *Wrestling with Moses: How Jane Jacobs Took On New York's Master Builder and Transformed the American City* (Random House, 2009), 186.

3. Richard H. Thaler and Cass R. Sunstein, *Nudge: Improving Decisions about Health, Wealth and Happiness* (Penguin Books, 2009), 60.

4. Ibid., 3, 6.

5. David Leonhardt, "The Battle Over Taxing Sodas," *New York Times*, May 20, 2010.

6. Gregory Mankiw, "Can a Soda Tax Save Us From Ourselves?" *New York Times*, June 4, 2010.

7. Since there is not enough money to go around, anti-smoking proponents are already worried that federal dollars will be shifted to anti-obesity stratagems. In 2010, the federal government spent $722 million on tobacco control and research and $821 million on obesity control and research. Duff Wilson, "Tobacco Funds Shrink as Obesity Fight Intensifies," *New York Times*, July 27, 2010.

8. New York State records showed that "of some 13,000 allegations of abuse in 2009 in state-operated and licensed homes, fewer than 5 per cent were referred to law enforcement." Danny Hakim, "At State-Run Homes, Abuse and Impunity," *New York Times*, March 12, 2011. It is absolute nonsense that all those who are vulnerable and in need of help must be shielded from citizen attention for their own good. Since when are government employees or those accredited by government the only ones we should rely on? Of course, there will always be non-professional volunteers who cause trouble, but to assume that those in the ranks of public unions or with professional credentials are superior in their everyday performance is to shut out too many with talent and discretion who can help out those in need. Government cannot afford, in the literal sense, to exclude such folks. To think that government standards should leave out so many is foolish given the economic times that we are going through.

9. This is already required in New York City for those fast food businesses with 15 outlets or more in the City. Thaler and Sunstein, *Nudge*, 262.

10. Ibid., 209–216.

11. Such spaces can also be transformed into community gardens providing "after-school programs for children, activities for the elderly, and a resource for food banks and homeless shelters." www.lgc.org/freepub/docs/community_design/. . ./community_gardens.pdf, accessed April 28, 2011.

12. Theodore Roszak went even further by suggesting tax deductions "for the value of the time" that an individual taxpayer "contributes to volunteer work." It is what Roszak calls "a shadow wage." Roszak, *The Making of an Elder Culture: Reflections on the Future of America's Most Audacious Generation* (New Society Publishers, 2009), 93.

13. As a model, the Hampton Youth Civic Engagement project in Hampton, Virginia has engaged young people in contributing their ideas on local policing, school reform, and job training with students taking charge of these subjects as adults learn from them, not the other way around. www.hampton.gov/for youth/youth_youth.html, accessed April 28, 2011.

14. There are always tax deductions, of course, that can stimulate all kinds of giving, but given the current revenue shortfall of governments, new deductions are not likely.

15. My September 11 edited recollections here appeared in a piece of mine: "Public Grieving and Public Thinking," *Higher Education Exchange*, 2002, 6–12.

16. Daniel J. Wakin, "At Ground Zero, Gospel and Giving," *New York Times*, December 1, 2001.

17. I was reminded of these essential questions when reading Bent Flyvbjerg's *Making Social Science Matter: Why Social Inquiry Fails and How It Can Succeed Again* (Cambridge University Press, 2001), 6.

18. "It is because every individual knows so little and, in particular, because we rarely know which of us knows best that we trust the independent and competitive efforts of many to induce the emergence of what we shall want when we see it." Frederick Hayek, *The Constitution of Liberty* (University of Chicago Press, Phoenix edition, 1978), 192.

19. James C. Scott, *Seeing Like a State* (Yale University Press, 1998), 316–317. As a Pasadena mayor once said: "We don't need your input . . . we need your help in solving problems." Daniel Kemmis, *The Good City and the Good Life* (Houghton Mifflin, 1995), 193.

20. Cass Sunstein, *Republic.com* (Princeton University Press, 2002), 39.

21. I already noted earlier that the metaphor of maps in their heads comes from William Schambra. See Cynthia Gibson, "Citizens at the Center," *Case Foundation* (2006): 23.

22. John McKnight, *The Careless Society: Community and Its Counterfeits* (Basic Books, 1995).

23. The objective/subjective distinction is made by Herbert A. Simon in "Human Nature in Politics," *American Political Science Review* 79 (1985): 293–304.

24. David Weinberger goes even further and sees the advantage of a never-ending tinkering with problems which goes beyond deliberation. It is the trial and error process when we put what we have learned together into various forms of action. Quoting with approval Tim Falconer, a Web consultant, "It's better to do something and tweak it for the rest of your life than to get thirty people into a room to figure out everything you're ever going to need." David Weinberger, *Everything is Miscellaneous* (Times Books, 2007), 193.

25. David Mathews, remarks when discussing community politics (date unknown).

26. "Breathtaking media abundance lives side by side with serious shortages in reporting." "A Federal Study Finds that Local Reporting Has Waned," *New York Times*, June 9, 2011.

27. Matthew Hindman, *The Myth of Digital Democracy* (Princeton University Press, 2009). There are, however, numerous websites that either host or convene online deliberation. Edith Manosevitch, "Mapping the Practice of Online Deliberation," A Report for the Media and Democracy Workgroup of the Kettering Foundation, July 2009.

28. Chris Anderson, *The Long Tail: Why the Future of Business Is Selling Less of More* (Hyperion, 2006), 30.

29. Alex S. Jones, *Losing the News: The Future of the News That Feeds Democracy* (Oxford University Press, 2009), 184. Jones sees "a broad populous awash in opinion, spin, and propaganda." 221.

30. Leonard Kitt, *National Civic Review* (Fall 2004), 49–50.

31. Much of what I learned about public journalism came from Jay Rosen, a professor of journalism at New York University, who was one of its intellectual leaders. Jay has moved on to a website, PressThink, which he thinks of as "the ghost of democracy in the media machine." http://pressthink.org/about/, accessed April 28, 2011.

32. Take the example of New York City government that offers an online "self-directed" volunteer service mechanism that provides downloadable toolkits for those who don't have the time or inclination to connect to a formal volunteer program. wwwnycservice.or/create_event.php. NYC government also took a full-page ad in the *New York Times*: "Everybody's Got Something to Offer. Skill, Time, Passion, Energy . . . "It's your blank and it can be anything." Advertisement, December 12, 2009.

33. And besides online news outlets, there are many personal websites and social media pages where as Clay Shirky puts it: "People like to consume media . . . but they also like to produce it ('Look what I've made') and they like to share it ('Look what I found.')." Clay Shirky, *Here Comes Everybody: The Power of Organizing Without Organizations* (Penguin Press, 2008), 104. Yes, I know there is an awful lot of preening online that goes nowhere, but new social practices can be sustained and enhanced when there are enough of us who announce, "Look what *we* made."

34. Wendell Berry calls this "solving for pattern" where one "solution . . . addresses multiple problems" which can be the symptom of a systems failure. Paul Hawken cites Berry in *Blessed Unrest: How the Largest Movement in the World Came into Being and Why No One Saw It Coming* (Viking, 2007), 178. Systems failure is certainly what we're dealing with when government cannot solve social problems for us and we fail to do it ourselves.

Selected Bibliography

Abrahamson, Eric and David H. Freedman. *A Perfect Mess: The Hidden Benefits of Disorder; How Crammed Closets, Cluttered Offices, and On-the-Fly Planning Make the World a Better Place.* Little, Brown, 2006.

Anderson, Chris. *The Long Tail: Why the Future of Business Is Selling Less of More.* Hyperion, 2006.

Axelrod, Robert and Michael D. Cohen. *Harnessing Complexity: Organizational Implications of a Scientific Frontier.* Free Press, 1999.

Ball, Philip. *Critical Mass: How One Thing Leads to Another.* Farrar, Straus and Giroux, 2004.

Barber, Benjamin. *Strong Democracy: Participatory Politics for a New Age.* University of California Press, 1984.

Behn, Robert D. "Management by Groping Along." *Journal of Policy Analysis and Management* 7, no. 4 (1988): 643–663.

Bellah, Robert N., Richard Madsen, William M. Sullivan, Ann Swidler, and Steven M. Tipton. *Habits of the Heart: Individualism and Commitment in American Life.* University of California Press, 1985.

Bellah, Robert N., Richard Madsen, Steven M. Tipton, and William M. Sullivan. *The Good Society.* Knopf, 1991.

Bishop, Bill. *The Big Sort: Why the Clustering of Like-Minded Americans Is Tearing Us Apart.* Houghton Mifflin, 2008.

Blau, Melinda, and Karen L. Fingerman. *Consequential Strangers: The Power of People Who Don't Seem to Matter . . . but Really Do.* W. W. Norton, 2009.

Bledstein, Burton J. *The Culture of Professionalism: The Middle Class and the Development of Higher Education in America.* W. W. Norton, 1978.

Boorstin, Daniel. *Democracy and Its Discontents: Reflections on Everyday America.* Random House, 1974.

Bornstein, David. *How to Change the World: Social Entrepreneurs and the Power of New Ideas*. Oxford University Press, 2004.

Boyte, Harry C. "Public Work: Civic Populism versus Technocracy in Higher Education." *Agent of Democracy: Higher Education and the HEX Journey*, ed. David W. Brown and Deborah Witte, 79–102. Kettering Foundation Press, 2008.

Braun, Eva. *Paradoxes of Education in a Republic*. University of Chicago Press, 1979.

Brint, Steven. *In An Age of Experts: The Changing Roles of Professionals in Politics and Public Life*. Princeton University Press, 1994.

Brooks, Victor D. *Boomers: The Cold-War Generation Grows Up*. Ivan R. Dee, 2009.

Brown, David W. "Cooperation among Strangers." An Occasional Paper of the Kettering Foundation, 1992.

Brown, David W. "The Journey of a Recovering Professional." *Higher Education Exchange*, 2008.

Brown, David W. *Organization Smarts: Portable Skills for Professionals Who Want to Get Ahead*. Amacom, 2002.

Brown, David W. "Professional Virtue." *Change,* November/December 1985.

Brown, David W. "Public Grieving and Public Thinking." *Higher Education Exchange*, 2002.

Brown, David W. *When Strangers Cooperate: Using Social Conventions to Govern Ourselves*. Free Press, 1995

Brown, John Seely, and Paul Duguid. *The Social Life of Information*. Harvard Business School Press, 2002.

Brufee, Kenneth A. *Collaborative Learning: Higher Education, Interdependence, and the Authority of Knowledge*. Johns Hopkins University Press, 1993.

Carr, Nicholas. *The Shallows: What the Internet Is Doing to Our Brains*. W. W. Norton, 2010.

Chong, Dennis. *Collective Action and the Civil Rights Movement*. University of Chicago Press, 1991.

Clippinger, John Henry. *A Crowd of One: The Future of Individual Identity*. Public Affairs, 2007.

Collins, Randall. *The Credentialed Society: An Historical Sociology of Education and Stratification*. Academic Press, 1979.

Cremin, Lawrence A. *Public Education*. Basic Books, 1976.

Crenson, Matthew A. and Benjamin Ginsberg. *Downsizing Democracy: How America Sidelined Its Citizens and Privatized Its Public*. Johns Hopkins University Press, 2004.

Crick, Bernard. *In Defense of Politics*. 2nd ed. University of Chicago Press, 1972.

Croker, Richard. *The Boomer Century: How America's Most Influential Generation Changed Everything*. Springboard Press, 2007.

Darnton, Robert. *The Case for Books: Past, Present, and Future*. Public Affairs, 2009.

Doherty, Brian. *Radical for Capitalism: A Freewheeling History of the Modern American Libertarian Movement*. Public Affairs, 2007.

Ellickson, Robert C. *Order Without Law: How Neighbors Settle Disputes*. Harvard University Press, 1991.

Elster, Jon. *The Cement of Society: A Study of Social Order*. Cambridge University Press, 1989.

Elster, Jon. *Nuts and Bolts for the Social Sciences*. Cambridge University Press, 1989.

Evans, Sara M. and Harry C. Boyte. *Free Spaces: The Sources of Democratic Change in America*. Harper & Row, 1986.

Fine, Allison. *Momentum: Igniting Social Change in the Connected Age*. Jossey-Bass, 2006.

Fischer, Claude S. *Made in America: A Social History of American Culture and Character*. University of Chicago Press, 2010.

Flacks, Richard. *Making History: The American Left and the American Mind*. Columbia University Press, 1988.

Flint, Anthony. *Wrestling with Moses: How Jane Jacobs Took On New York's Master Builder and Transformed the American City*. Random House, 2009.

Florida, Richard. *The Rise of the Creative Class: And How It's Transforming Work, Leisure, Community and Everyday Life*. Basic Books, 2002.

Flyvbjerg, Bent. *Making Social Science Matter: Why Social Inquiry Fails and How It Can Succeed Again*. Cambridge University Press, 2001.

Forester, John. *The Deliberative Practitioner: Encouraging Participatory Planning Processes*. MIT Press, 2000.

Freedman, David H. *Wrong: Why Experts* Keep Failing Us and How to Know When Not to Trust Them: Scientists, Finance Wizards, Doctors, Relationship Gurus, Celebrity CEOs, High-Powered Consultants, Health Officials, and More*. Little, Brown, 2010.

Freedman, Marc. *The Big Shift: Navigating the New Stage Beyond Midlife*. Public Affairs, 2011.

Friedman, Thomas L. *The World Is Flat: A Brief History of the Twenty-First Century*. Farrar, Straus and Giroux, 2005.

Gladwell, Malcolm. *Outliers: The Story of Success*. Little, Brown, 2008.

Gladwell, Malcolm. *The Tipping Point: How Little Things Can Make a Big Difference*. Little, Brown, 2000.

Granovetter, Mark S. "The Strength of Weak Ties." *American Journal of Sociology* 8, no. 6, 1973.

Hardin, Russell. *Collective Action*. Johns Hopkins University Press, 1982.

Harwood, Richard C., and John A. Creighton. "The Organization-First Approach." *Harwood Institute for Public Innovation*, 2009.

Hawken, Paul. *Blessed Unrest: How the Largest Movement in the World Came into Being and Why No One Saw It Coming.* Viking, 2007.

Hayek, Frederick. *The Constitution of Liberty.* University of Chicago Press, Phoenix edition, 1978.

Hechter, Michael. *Principles of Group Solidarity.* University of California Press, 1987.

Hindman, Matthew. *The Myth of Digital Democracy.* Princeton University Press, 2009.

Hirschman, Albert O. *Exit, Voice, Loyalty: Responses to Decline in Firms, Organizations, and States.* Harvard University Press, 1970.

Hirschman, Albert O. *Shifting Involvements: Private Interest and Public Action.* Princeton University Press, 1982.

Holland, John. *Emergence: From Chaos to Order.* Addison Wesley, 1998.

Holland, John. *Hidden Order: How Adaptation Builds Complexity.* Addison Wesley, 1995.

Jacobs, Jane. *The Death and Life of Great American Cities.* Vintage Books, 1961.

Johnson, Steven. *Emergence: The Connected Lives of Ants, Brains, Cities and Software.* Scribner, 2001.

Jones, Alex. *Losing the News: The Future of the News That Feeds Democracy.* Oxford University Press, 2009.

Keen, Andrew. *The Cult of the Amateur: How Today's Internet is Killing Our Culture.* Doubleday/Currency, 2007.

Kemmis, Dan. *The Good City and the Good Life: Renewing the Sense of Community.* Houghton Mifflin, 1995.

Kluger, Jeffrey. *Simplexity: Why Simple Things Become Complex (and How Complex Things Can Be Made Simple).* Hyperion, 2008.

Lanier, Jaron. *You Are Not a Gadget: A Manifesto.* Knopf, 2010.

Leighninger, Matt. *The Next Form of Democracy: How Expert Rule is Giving Way to Shared Governance . . . and Why Politics Will Never Be the Same.* Vanderbilt University Press, 2006.

Lewis, David. *Convention: A Philosophical Study.* Harvard University Press, 1969.

Lindblom, Charles. *Inquiry and Change: The Troubled Attempt to Shape Society.* Yale University Press, 1990.

Lindblom, Charles. *Politics and Markets: The World's Political-Economic Systems.* Basic Books, 1997.

Lindblom, Charles, and David K. Cohen. *Usable Knowledge: Social Science and Social Problem Solving.* Yale University Press, 1979.

Macedo, Stephen, ed. *Deliberative Politics: Essays on Democracy and Disagreement.* Oxford University Press, 1999.

Macedo, Stephen, with Yvette Alex-Assensoh, Jeffrey M. Berry, Michael Brintnall, David E. Campbell, Luis Ricardo Fraga, Archon Fung, William A. Galston,

Christopher F. Karpowitz, Margaret Levi, Meira Levinson, Keena Lipsitz, Richard G. Niemi, Robert D. Putnam, Wendy M. Rahn, Rob Reich, Robert R, Rodgers, Todd Swanstrom, and Katherine Cramer Walsh. *Democracy at Risk: How Political Choices Undermine Citizen Participation and What We Can Do About It.* Brookings Institution Press, 2005.

Manosevitch, Edith. "Mapping the Practice of Online Deliberation." A Report for the Media and Democracy Workgroup of the Kettering Foundation. July 2009.

Mathews, David. *Politics for People: Finding a Responsible Public Voice.* University of Illinois Press, 1994.

Mathews, David. "The Public and the Public Schools: The Coproduction of Education." *Phi Delta Kappan,* April 2008.

Mathews, David. *Reclaiming Public Education by Reclaiming Our Democracy.* Kettering Foundation Press, 2006.

McKnight, John. *The Careless Society: Community and Its Counterfeits.* Basic Books, 1995.

McKnight, John. "Do No Harm," *Social Policy* 20, no. 1 (Summer 1989): 5–15.

McMillan, John. *Reinventing the Bazaar: A Natural History of Markets.* W. W. Norton, 2002.

Merelman, Richard M. *Making Something of Ourselves: On Culture and Politics in the United States.* University of California Press, 1984.

Mill, John Stuart. *On Liberty.* Appleton-Century-Crofts, 1947.

Mindell, David. *The Evolving World: Evolution in Everyday Life.* Harvard University Press, 2006.

Morone, James A. *The Democratic Wish: Popular Participation and the Limits of American Government.* Rev. ed. Yale University Press, 1998.

Oliver, Pamela, and Gerald Maxwell. "The Paradox of Group Size in Collective Action: A Theory of the Critical Mass II." *Sociological Review* 53 (1988): 1–8.

Olson, Mancur. *The Logic of Collective Action: Public Goods and the Theory of Groups.* Harvard University Press, 1980.

Olson, Mancur. *The Rise and Decline of Nations: Economic Growth, Stagflation, and Social Rigidities.* Yale University Press, 1982.

Ostrom, Eleanor. *Governing the Commons: The Evolution of Institutions for Collective Action.* Cambridge University Press, 1990.

Palmer, Parker. *The Active Life: Wisdom of Work, Creativity, and Caring.* Harper & Row, 1990.

Pitkin, Hannah. "Justice: On Relating Private and Public." *Political Theory* 9, no. 3 (1981): 327–351.

Polletta, Francesca. *Freedom Is an Endless Meeting: Democracy in American Social Movements.* University of Chicago Press, 2002.

Polletta, Francesca. *It Was Like a Fever: Storytelling in Protest and Politics.* University of Chicago Press, 2006.

Postman, Neil. *Amusing Ourselves to Death: Public Discourse in the Age of Show Business.* Penguin Books, 1985.

Putnam, Robert. *Bowling Alone: The Collapse and Revival of American Community.* Simon & Schuster, 2000.

Raymond, Eric S. *The Cathedral and the Bazaar: Musing on Linux and Open Sources by an Accidental Revolutionary.* O'Reilly, 2001.

Reich, Robert B. *The Work of Nations: Preparing Ourselves for 21st-Century Capitalism.* Vintage Books, 1992.

Resnick, Mitchell. *Turtles, Termites, and Traffic Jams: Explorations in Massively Parallel Microworlds.* MIT Press, 1994.

Rheingold, Howard. *Smart Mobs: The Next Social Revolution.* Basic Books, 2002.

Ridley, Matt. *The Origins of Virtue: Human Instincts and the Evolution of Cooperation.* Viking, 1996.

Rorty, Richard. *Achieving Our Country: Leftist Thought in Twentieth-Century America.* Harvard University Press, 1998.

Rorty, Richard. *Consequences of Pragmatism* University of Minnesota Press, 1982.

Rosenbaum, Nancy L. *Membership and Morals: The Personal Uses of Pluralism in America.* Princeton University Press, 2000.

Roszak, Theodore. *The Making of an Elder Culture: Reflections on the Future of America's Most Audacious Generation.* New Society Publishers, 2009.

Sandel, Michael. *Democracy's Discontent: America In Search of a Public Philosophy.* Belknap/Harvard University Press, 1996.

Sandel, Michael. *Liberalism and the Limits of Justice.* Cambridge University Press, 1982.

Sandel, Michael. "Political Theory of the Procedural Republic." In *The Power of Public Ideas*, ed. Robert Reich. Bellinger, 109–121. 1988.

Schelling, Thomas C. *Micromotives and Macrobehavior.* W. W. Norton, 1978.

Schon, Donald A. *The Reflective Practitioner: How Professionals Think in Action.* Basic Books, 1983.

Scott, James C. *Seeing Like a State: How Certain Schemes to Improve the Human Condition Have Failed.* Yale University Press, 1998.

Seabright, Paul. *The Company of Strangers: A Natural History of Economic Life.* Princeton University Press, 2004.

Shenkman, Rick. *Just How Stupid Are We? Facing the Truth about the American Voter.* Basic Books, 2008.

Shirky, Clay. *Cognitive Surplus: Creativity and Generosity in a Connected Age.* Penguin Press, 2010.

Shirky, Clay. *Here Comes Everybody: The Power of Organizing Without Organizations.* Penguin Press, 2008.

Skocpol, Theda. *Diminshed Democracy: From Membership to Management in American Civic Life.* University of Oklahoma Press, 2003.

Slater, Philip. *The Pursuit of Loneliness: American Culture at the Breaking Point.* Beacon Press, 1970.

Smith, Walker, and Ann Clurman. *Generation Ageless: How Baby Boomers Are Changing the Way We Live Today . . . and They're Just Getting Started.* Collins, 2007.

Stone, Deborah. *The Samaritan's Dilemma: Should Government Help Your Neighbor?* Nation Books, 2008.

Sugden, Robert. *The Economics of Rights, Co-operation and Welfare.* Basil Blackwell, 1986.

Sullivan, William M. *Reconstructing Public Philosophy.* University of California Press, 1982.

Sullivan, William M. *Work and Integrity: The Crisis and Promise of Professionalism in America.* Harper Collins, 1995.

Sunstein, Cass. *Republic.com.* Princeton University Press, 2002.

Sunstein, Cass. "Social Norms and Social Rules." *Columbia Law Review*, 1996.

Surowiecki, James. *The Wisdom of Crowds: Why the Many Are Smarter Than the Few and How Collective Wisdom Shapes Business, Economics, Societies, and Nations.* Doubleday, 2004.

Taylor, Michael. "Rationality and Revolutionary Collective Action." In *Rationality and Revolution,* ed. Michael Taylor, 63–97. Studies in Marxism and Social Theory. Cambridge University Press, 1982.

Tetlock, Philip. *Expert Political Judgment: How Good Is It? How Can We Know?* Princeton University Press, 2005.

Thaler, Richard H., and Cass R. Sunstein. *Nudge: Improving Decisions about Health, Wealth and Happiness.* Penguin Books, 2009.

Tocqueville, Alexis de. *Democracy in America.* Ed. J.P. Mayer. Doubleday, 1969.

Ullmann-Margalit, Edna. *The Emergence of Norms.* Oxford University Press, 1977.

Waldrop, M. Mitchell. *Complexity: The Emerging Science at the Edge of Order and Chaos.* Simon & Schuster, 1992.

Warren, Mark R. *Dry Bones Rattling: Community Building to Revitalize American Democracy.* Princeton University Press, 2001.

Watts, Duncan. *Six Degrees: The Science of a Connected Age.* W.W. Norton, 2003.

Weick, Karl. *Making Sense of the Organization.* Blackwell Publishers, 2001.

Weick, Karl. "Managerial Thought in the Context of Action." In *The Executive Mind,* ed. S. Srivastava, 221–242. Jossey Bass, 1983.

Weick, Karl. *Sensemaking in Organizations.* Sage Publications, 1995.

Weinberger, David. *Everything is Miscellaneous: The Power of the New Digital Disorder.* Times Books, 2007.

Wheatley, Margaret and Deborah Frieze. "Using Emergence to Take Social Innovations to Scale." *Kettering Review,* Summer 2009, 34–38.

Whitehead, Alfred North. *Science and the Modern World.* Free Press, 1967.

Whyte, William H. *City: Rediscovering the Center.* Anchor Books, 1988.

Wiebe, Robert H. *Self-Rule: A Cultural History of American Democracy.* University of Chicago Press, 1995.

Wuthnow, Robert. *Loose Connections: Joining Together in America's Fragmented Communities.* Harvard University Press, 1998.

Index

About the Author

DAVID WARFIELD BROWN has experienced the public world from various vantage points as a lawyer on Wall Street, chief of staff on Capitol Hill, state commissioner in New York, deputy mayor of New York City, public authority board member, professor at Yale and the New School, president of Blackburn College, author of two previous books (*When Strangers Cooperate*, Free Press, 1995; *Organization Smarts*, Amacom, 2002), and coeditor of two more (*Agent of Democracy*, Kettering Foundation Press, 2008; *A Different Kind of Politics*, Kettering Foundation Press, 2009). Brown is the ongoing editor of Kettering's *Higher Education Exchange*, an annual publication, and his primary research interest is the social dimensions of problem solving.